Praise for *The Wall Around Your Heart*

"No matter how someone else has injured you—betrayal, abuse, abandonment, manipulation, neglect, physical harm, exploitation—*The Wall Around Your Heart* will be a balm of healing, because no injury is too great for Jesus to mend. If you are drowning in pain or bitterness or shock from a broken relationship, start on the first page of this book and set it down at the end healed."

— Jen Hatmaker, best-selling author of *Interrupted* and *7: An Experimental Mutiny Against Excess*

"Nobody escapes life without a wounded heart. Mary knows how deep the valley of relational hurt can go, leaving us with a half-hearted ability to love. She shares with unmasked clarity how Jesus can heal those relational riffs, so you won't stay walled off from God's joy."

— John Burke, author of *No Perfect People Allowed*

"One of Christianity's premier authors has crafted a powerful healing balm for true Jesus followers."

— Frank Viola, author of *God's Favorite Place on Earth*, frankviola.org

"When people let us down—and they will—the Lord's Prayer serves as a map on the highway to healing. In *The Wall Around Your Heart*, Mary DeMuth takes readers on a journey of masterful storytelling, biblically sound content, and road-tested experience to show them how. Highly recommended!"

— Sandra Glahn, author of Coffee Cup Bible Studies series

"I can't think of a woman I know who wouldn't benefit from the wisdom and hope to be found in Mary DeMuth's latest book *The Wall Around My Heart*. The way she mines the Lord's Prayer for healing truths is ingenious. As always, DeMuth writes with the kind of rare authenticity that draws you in and keeps you turning pages. You can't help but be changed by the message in this book, and you'll never pray the Lord's Prayer the same way again."

— Heather Kopp, author of *Sober Mercies: How Love Caught Up with a Christian Drunk*

"Mary DeMuth offers here an invitation to habituate the Lord's Prayer as a healing balm to the fractured and broken places of the spirit. Her frank and matter-of-fact turn of phrase journeys the reader through the depths of ache and up into the heights of joy. DeMuth whispers into the soul the gospel of peace, the promise of a Christ in whom all the fractured are made whole."

— Preston Yancey, author of seeprestonblog.com

"I love how my friend Mary DeMuth uses the stories of her life to tell the stories of God's work in our lives. She did it for me today in *The Wall Around Your Heart*, touching my heart with tender reminders of God's love and grace. Mary weaves the powerful beauty of the Lord's Prayer with the challenges of hurtful relationships and events, creating an exquisite tapestry of healing and restoration and hope."

— Judy Douglass, author, speaker, encourager, director of Women's Resources, Cru

"This is a fallen world. Others hurt us and we make our own bad choices. So how do we survive the wreckage of broken relationships? How do we salvage our identity when we've found ourselves at the bottom of the pile? Mary DeMuth knows the answers to these questions because she's lived them. If you long for healing and wholeness after relational heartbreak, walk with Mary through these pages. She'll help you recover your identity, learn to trust again, and find the beauty in worship amidst it all."

— Susie Larson, author, speaker, radio host

"The Body of Christ is beautiful, and I'm glad to limp along with them in this crazy journey of faith. Along the way, I sometimes step on someone's toes, or someone steps on mine. Mary has written this guidebook to help successfully navigate those seasons where I'm tempted to hold a grudge and give up on the Body of Christ. Using the Lord's Prayer—each line—as a prompt, I'm reminded of God's desire to heal and comfort me in each of my relationships; especially the ones in which I have been deeply hurt, and even broken."

— Deidra Riggs, writer, deidrariggs.com; managing editor of TheHighCalling.org

"Life hurts us, we feel pain, and we struggle. . . . So what do we do with hurting lives and raw situations? . . . Mary says, 'It's counterintuitive to praise God when people hurt us, but it's the best thing we can do!' . . . This book is full of resilient hope and radiant healing. . . . Every page beats with life and fresh hope!"

— Johnny Douglas, Anglican pastor

The Wall Around Your Heart

How Jesus Heals You When Others Hurt You

MARY DEMUTH

NELSON BOOKS

Published in Nashville, Tennessee, by Nelson Books, an imprint of Thomas Nelson. Nelson Books and Thomas Nelson are registered trademarks of HarperCollins Christian Publishing, Inc.

Thomas Nelson, Inc., titles may be purchased in bulk for educational, business, fund-raising, or sales promotional use. For information, please e-mail SpecialMarkets@ThomasNelson.com.

Published in association with the literary agency of Fedd & Company, Inc., Post Office Box 341973, Austin, TX 78734.

Library of Congress Cataloging-in-Publication Data

DeMuth, Mary E., 1967–
The wall around your heart : how Jesus heals you when others hurt you / Mary DeMuth.
pages cm
Includes bibliographical references.
ISBN 978-1-4002-0521-9
1. Lord's prayer—Criticism, interpretation, etc. 2. Spiritual healing. 3. Suffering—Religious aspects—Christianity. I. Title.
BV230.D36 2013
226.9'606—dc23 2013009819

Printed in the United States of America

13 14 15 16 17 RRD 6 5 4 3 2 1

To Twilla Fontenot, the most openhearted person I know. I want to live, laugh, and love like you when I grow up.

Contents

Introduction

The Fortress Heart

I SEE WALLS NEARLY EVERYWHERE. DEVASTATION AND BITTERNESS in the aftermath of relationship blowups. Folks walking zombie-like after friends betray. People leaving churches because of underhanded remarks. Friends, years in the making, departing as enemies. Hurt people barricading themselves from ever having to feel relational pain again, discovering instead the angst of loneliness behind the barrier. People holding tightly to control, only to see their relational worlds spin into chaos. Others who cannot focus on a task because of all the conflict hollering around them.

Walls aren't pretty.

But they're real.

In talking to friends in painful situations (and having been all the people I listed above), I've discovered a pathway through the devastation. It's not simple or simplistic, but it's truthful.

And it involves prayer.

Not passive prayer, where you send out a lethargic "Hey, help me," in the midst of an argument.

Not wishful thinking prayer, where you half hope for a different outcome.

Not even yelling prayer, where you rail at injustice.

It's the type of prayer that Jesus modeled, lived, breathed. Of all the people on this earth who had cause to wall off His heart against those who hurt Him (that would be the entire world), He had cause. And yet He loved people who ignored Him. He interacted with betrayers. He offered grace to those who violated His laws. He dignified outcasts. He engaged Himself in the very world that put Him to death. Jesus is our example of openhearted living, of exhibiting wild love that dared to wash the feet of Judas, who betrayed Him, of reinstating Peter, who denied Him thrice. Jesus, in His divine irresistibility, welcomed all, loved all, endured all.

So when Jesus prayed, He gave His friends insight into how He walked so fully alive. Tucked within His prayer are secrets to withstanding conflict, letting go of turmoil, and seeing God in His proper light.

We find solace and relief and help in the aftermath of

painful relationships by following the road map of the Lord's Prayer. We've heard the prayer a thousand upon a thousand times. We've memorized it. Recited it. Listened to it. Sung it. But have we considered the power of Jesus' words in this prayer and how it perfectly relates to broken relationships, interpersonal hardship, or even abuse?

I'd like you to read the prayer from the New Living Translation. As you do, think about the people in your life with whom you've experienced conflict or devastation. Picture each one. Examine your heart. Has bitterness taken root? Have you walled off your emotions from that person? Do you have a physical reaction when the person's name is mentioned? Or maybe you've had difficulty with a group of people. A Bible study at church? Christian leaders? Your entire family of origin? Think on these people as you read:

> *Pray like this:*
> *Our Father in heaven,*
> *may your name be kept holy.*
> *May your Kingdom come soon.*
> *May your will be done on earth,*
> *as it is in heaven.*
> *Give us today the food we need,*
> *and forgive us our sins,*
> *as we have forgiven those who sin against us.*
> *And don't let us yield to temptation,*
> *but rescue us from the evil one. (Matt. 6:9–13)*

If you're like me, upon first reading, you probably hone in on the forgiveness element of the prayer. Yes, we must forgive our enemies and those who sin against us. Typically people who hurt us aren't vague entities. They aren't governments or far-off institutions. The ones who cut into our hearts, severing parts of us, are people we know. They hurt us more deeply because of the closeness we've felt. In light of that, forgiveness takes on a deeper meaning.

There's more to this prayer than forgiveness, although if you experience that from the prayer, you'll be on your way to a whole, free life. The framework of this book camps around the eleven phrases in this prayer. It represents everything I've learned in the past thirty years as a Jesus-loving disciple who makes every kind of relational mistake.

As I write these words, even now I'm haunted by one relationship gone askew. I picture my friend's face, hear her laughter, remember our times of prayer, and consider how we discovered joy together. And I ache in the distance now. I can't seem to fix the problem, nor do I discern its root. I have to rest in God's sovereign, perfect plan and trust that He will work this for good someday. I have to let Him examine my heart, probing the ways I protect myself and wall myself away from people who cause pain. I have to admit that I'm the problem. And even then, I have to offer myself grace, knowing that sometimes you do everything you can do, only to move on in the rhythm of life, letting some relationships go.

So I don't come to this book with a feeling of triumphalism. If anything, I trumpet my weakness, my many petty sins (and great ones too). I write these words because I've experienced Jesus—on the pages of my Bible, in the lives of my friends, in the deepest parts of my soul. When Jesus gave us the most important boiled-down commandments, He made life quite clear, didn't He? Love God. Love others. That's it. How we do both is how we'll be remembered on earth and the sweet hereafter. I fail at both. I love things. I love my reputation. I love control. I love harmony at any cost. I love ease. I love food. I love success. And I don't often run to prayer.

The greatest challenge of my life is choosing to commune with God with everything I am, learning to receive His wild but abundant love, then flinging it joyfully in people's direction. And in the midst of that, I've understood the importance of settling my soul, quieting my condemning mind, and seeing myself as one who is embraced and favored in God's sight. Why do we live in the paradox that if we are to love others, we must accept God's love for us? It's the river of life, flowing from within, that God pours inside us and ignites the unction to pour into others.

Simply said, we can't love if we're not loved.

We can't give from emptiness.

Which is why loving others is not a sheer act of grumbly will. It's not something we check off our "love people" to-do list. It's messy. It's tenacious. It has to come from the authenticity of our hearts, where Jesus has dynamically changed us.

My heart for you in this journey we'll be taking together is this: be loved. Be wildly and audaciously loved. Give what you receive. See others as Jesus sees you. Settle your worth. Rest in God's compassion. And as you choose to believe His favor, your life won't be able to help spilling love, compassion, and forgiveness to everyone you meet.

The Lord's Prayer is our treasure map. The obstacles are our hearts and the pain inflicted by others. But the outcome will be freedom, joy, peace, healing, hope, and our fortress wall broken down.

"Pray Like This"

Pray First

JESUS STARTED HIS FAMOUS PRAYER WITH THREE WORDS: "PRAY like this." Not gossip like this. Not tell everyone else the other person's issues like this. Not stew on the issue until your heart embitters like this. Not grumble like this. Not avoid like this.

"Pray like this."

I'm typing these words after a hellacious bout of stress that's toppled our family and sent me careening for answers. Our youngest daughter experienced scary health problems, the kind that sent her to the hospital more than once. It almost seems counterintuitive to write those three one-syllable words.

Pray.

Like.

This.

So in whatever circumstance we walk, Jesus beckons us toward prayer, toward relationship with Him. The very essence of this prayer welcomes honesty, to let Jesus in on whatever stresses us out. Running to the Greek helps me (and makes my Greek-loving, theology-bent husband proud). The Greek word for "this" is *proseuchomai. Pro* means "to face or look toward." *Euchomai* translates "to declare out loud, express a wish" (I like that).[1] In the New Testament, the word is always used in reference to God, and it sounds like the word for "worship," *proskuneo.*[2] So when Jesus used this word, He communicated more than three words. We must speak to God face-to-face, sharing our hearts and burdens, and as we do, we choose to worship Him in the process. To let Him know how big He is in relation to our current pain.

But Jesus doesn't invite us only to Him in this prayer; He welcomes us into His community. I don't always run to others when painful circumstances squeeze life from me. I cocoon myself, cry, wallow, and give in to catatonic stares. I isolate myself. Although this recent trial has little to do with a painful relationship, the beckoning of Jesus remains the same. He wants to be a part of our pain, to walk alongside us through the bewilderment, to shoulder the burdens we pick up so quickly by ourselves. And He wants to invite us to community, so others can be His hands and feet when we can't feel or walk. His invitation in this prayer isn't simply to Him but to the family He created when He died on the cross and welcomed us into community.

Jesus welcomed me to Himself and to my husband (community) during a particularly difficult time in our marriage. I had a conversation with my husband about a couple we once knew. The husband had been chewing tobacco and hiding it from his wife. When she found out, she exploded. Although they were tentacled in the moment, the couple used that time of sheer honesty to start a new foundation in their relationship. I admired them, but I'm pretty sure I said, "Honey, if you ever do anything like that, I'll kill you." I said it with a smile. But my smile had teeth.

Flip forward in the DeMuth family album. For some reason, I couldn't use our minivan to go to the gym one morning, so I borrowed Patrick's truck. I needed something in the glove compartment. As I opened it, a little round can fell to the passenger's side floor. My heart fell with it. My husband was hiding his habit.

I wanted to yell. I envisioned a lot of ranting and storming about, arms flailing to the ceiling, voice attaining a high pitch. But instead I stopped in that moment, turned on the ignition, and drove to the gym. I stepped onto the treadmill, plugged in some worship music, and prayed like a crazy woman. Face forward, I let Jesus have every bit of me, every feeling of betrayal, every hot shred of anger, every gnarl of revenge. It helped that I ran fast and hard. My husband's deception, and my finding out without him first being honest, no longer felt larger than God. He would be with me. He would give me calm but firm words.

Since it had been early in the morning when I exercised,

my tobacco-chewing husband was asleep when I arrived home. I watched him for a minute, wondering if there were other unsolved mysteries between us. And then I crawled in next to him. I placed my arms around him and said, "I found your can of chew in the glove compartment. Want to tell me the story?"

Oddly, we had a civil conversation. I didn't explode. I'd been one of those wives who had secret fears, particularly this one after our friends had walked through it. I thought beforehand that I couldn't bear up under that kind of trickery. But I did. By God's sheer and available grace.

Patrick apologized. He felt relieved, actually, to be found out. And he kept chewing but no longer in secret. The power of the secret faded, and he kicked the habit without me nagging or ranting or threatening.

Please don't think me a saint in this story. There are plenty of other stories where I bent my anger, angled it right at my husband's heart in the grip of rage. But in this instance, I chose to "pray like this," and it made all the difference. I focused on Jesus. On that treadmill, I thought of the cross, how Jesus suffered innocently for the wrong we did. His suffering gave me an invitation for kinship with Him. Still, I felt betrayed, lied to, and deceived. The weight of my husband's sin felt hot and sticky, and I suffered under it.

But in giving every single thought to Jesus in that moment, I opened the door for healing in my marriage. I can easily see how that one instance could've ushered us down a destructive path. And I realized that if my husband could deceive me, I truly couldn't change him. The only thing I could control was my response when I found out. I won't stand before a holy God and be judged for others' sins. Only for my own.

We forget that sin tends to abound, to grow, to flourish in the midst of angry arguments, where we can blame someone for the terrible thing he or she did. Our ungodly or uncontrolled response can add more sin to the mix until it becomes a volcanic sinfest. By taking my anger to Jesus first, I settled my heart, gave it some space to process and grieve, and experienced an odd sense of peace.

We tend to wall off our hearts in the aftermath of pain. Praying this way is preventive; it prevents the walls before we take up bricks. Prayer is proactive, restorative, and rejuvenating. And it begins with Jesus—who He is. Shane Claiborne emphasized the action portion of prayer when he wrote, "I've learned that prayer is not just about trying to get God to do what we want God to do but about getting ourselves to do what God wants us to do. Training us to be the kind of people God wants us to be."[3]

At the genesis of the Lord's Prayer, we're reminded that we have to start somewhere after pain. What's essential? Why? And how can we begin to respond well?

Begin with Jesus

WE START OUR JOURNEY OF TRANSFORMATION WITH THE GOD-MAN who spoke the words of this prayer. Asking yourself *Who is Jesus?*—and being truthful in your answer—is the most important question you'll ever ask. Why? Because how we frame our answer determines how much we allow Him into our pain, whether past or present.

After a traumatic childhood, where God's name was a swear word, and my pleas to go to Sunday school were ignored, I had no idea how to begin with Jesus. I honestly didn't know He existed.

What I did know: something about me felt fundamentally broken. I had no safe place to talk through the devastation of my childhood, no one to tell about childhood rape at five or to talk about my father's death when I was ten. More than that, I believed I was a walking mistake, a fluke of a girl who shouldn't have been born, meant to be in the way—a nuisance. I didn't experience fond affection or nurturing. In almost every way, I lived alone, unable to rightly process the pain that others had inflicted my way. Had I never met Jesus, I'd have spent my entire life in reverse, reliving the aftermath year after year, learning clever ways to numb my pain, excite my life, or end it all.

In the eighth grade, the past caught up with me. I was a combustive mess, a volatile cocktail of unmet expectations, loneliness, anger, and fear. The actions of others piled on top of me, and I couldn't find hope in that darkness. I wanted to end my life.

Chances are, you've been in a place like that once or twice, where other people's actions have hijacked you. You're like Joseph from the book of Genesis whose brothers sold him into slavery. Through no fault of your own, you scratch around in an earthen pit, longing for rescue, only to be enslaved the moment someone pulls you from the hole. This is how people's lives venture into pain's path. They find short rescue only to live a lifetime enslaved to that pain.

I could not see out of the pit at fourteen years old. I didn't want to see out of it. I'd resigned myself to a sad life or no life at all.

But Jesus.

He had other plans. He's the One who rescued me from the pit of other people's abuse so I didn't have to live back then in the fulcrum of all that pain. A year later, I heard the simple story of Jesus, told from the Gospels. Every week, the Young Life leader enticed me with more. Jesus hugged outcasts. He turned things around for broken folks. He settled disputes. He told the self-important to calm down and start loving. He played.

I could nearly see the dirt beneath His nails, hear the tenderness in His voice, and discern His laughter as He loved. Jesus changed every single thing about me because He embodied the opposite of the oppressors in my life. Where they came to steal, Jesus gave me life. Where they pushed for my destruction, Jesus provided exuberance. Where their neglect pushed me further into myself, Jesus opened me up like a gift.

At fifteen years old, I could barely contain all the Jesus stories. So I asked Jesus to please rewrite my story. I gave Him joyful permission to deal with the villains in my life, heal me from untold stories, and bring out a sweeter denouement. And He did.

Anyone dealing with feeling stuck after relational pain must start with Jesus, our empathetic Savior. Consider what Jesus experienced by the very people He created:

- People mocked Him.
- They abandoned Him.
- They undressed Him.
- Friends rejected Him and His message.
- Even His disciples misunderstood Him.
- Several wanted Him to be someone He wasn't.
- Some spat on Him.
- Many disobeyed Him.
- Peter denied Him.
- Judas, one of His closest friends, exchanged His life for pocket change.
- Some took up stones to kill Him.
- Others believed they were better than He was.
- Religious people were wildly and terribly jealous of Him.
- Many left Him at the point He needed them most.

We begin with Jesus because He understands. He lived through hell-on-earth, experienced everything we'll experience, and came through victorious in the aftermath. Because of His amazing empathy, we no longer need to lose heart. He who asked us to "pray like this" knew that we'd need this prayer. He knew we'd experience heartache. And He knew we would need a Savior who would "get" us.

His sympathy reminds me of this passage: "Now that we know what we have—Jesus, this great High Priest with ready access to God—let's not let it slip through our fingers. We don't have a priest who is out of touch with our reality. He's been through weakness and testing, experienced it all—all but the sin. So let's walk right up to him and get what he is so ready to give. Take the mercy, accept the help" (Heb. 4:14–16 MSG).

To make it through to the other side of relational pain, we start with Jesus. And then we move to His affection.

Begin with His Affection

WE'D AVOID A LOT OF INSECURITY IF WE FULLY, WHOLLY BELIEVED IN God's wild affection for us. Once we've internalized that foundational truth, secure and loved, we begin to see that God also loves the people who have hurt us. But we cannot love our enemies until we see those twin truths: God loves me. God loves them.

In my late teens, a leader hurt me, discouraged me, and sent me reeling. Because this leader wore a ministry badge, the hurt felt even more cancerous. Isn't that how we are sometimes? We can excuse the shenanigans of others who don't know Jesus, but if the person is a Christian, particularly a leader, the pain feels deeper and harder and more perplexing. During this time as I nursed my bewilderment (and looking back on the story, I'm better able to see my dysfunction in our interchange), the leader experienced romance. I couldn't understand how anyone could love the leader. Why? How? All I could see was the blackness of the leader's sin, which made her all evil in my eyes. I defined her in absolutes, but I had absolutely no grace for her.

Immature and angry, I stewed about this for a month or two until I finally realized that Jesus deeply loved this woman. He died for her. He had fond affection for her heart, her dreams, her soul, her wherewithal. When I realized this, all my catastrophic thinking about how evil she was started to fade. I began to pray for her, see her in a different light, and eventually forgive her.

In another instance, I had an otherworldly anger toward the brothers who molested me when I was five years old. For my entire kindergarten year, they took me from my babysitter's house, pulled me into ravines and out-of-the-way places, and raped me. They asked their friends to join in. They threatened me.

"If you tell, you'll never, ever be able to have babies someday."

"If you tell, we'll kill your mother and father."

They pushed me down, placed dirty hands over my mouth so I couldn't scream, and did that awful, violating act. The only thing that rescued me that year was my ability to fake sleep and a providential move twenty miles away.

I could not see those boys in light of Jesus' love for them. For years.

But eventually grace crept into my heart.

I realized those boys learned that behavior somewhere,

whether they'd been abused by someone or found pornography that fueled their very real fantasies. I came to realize that they'd most likely been victims. And I thought about what would happen to people like that once they reached adulthood. Did they offend again? Tuck that awful stuff in a locked back closet of memory? Were they haunted by guilt? Once I explored those questions, I began to see Jesus' affection for those boys, now men. And honestly, if I saw them today, I would ask lots of questions, offer to pray, and tell them Jesus loves them. That's the work of Jesus, not me. Which is why we must begin with Jesus and His affection for the people who hurt us. And after we do that, our focus must shift heavenward.

Begin with Worship

IT'S COUNTERINTUITIVE TO PRAISE GOD WHEN PEOPLE HURT US. BUT it's the best thing we can do. When we were in ministry, Patrick and I endured deception, meanness, and undermining by people who were supposed to be Christian leaders. Some of the injury felt meaningless. We endured all of this while we walked through financial duress and culture shock, and our children had difficulty with demeaning teachers. On every level of our lives, we felt attacked. Many days all I wanted to do was stay in bed, never venturing out into the big, bad world. My capacity to bear more pain had been stretched to breaking.

The one thing that helped me through this time was a little ritual I practiced in the mornings. After we walked the kids to school or sometimes before, I jogged up the hill behind our home with my iPod tuned to worship. As I ran and listened to the words of songs extolling the beauty of God, renewal washed over me. Though my problems felt gargantuan, they shrank to their proper size in the light of God's greatness. The panic faded. The worry waned. And I found myself humming along to the melody while lavender fields and vineyards reminded me that God was a great Creator, and He was mindful of me, even when I felt small and buried beneath the sin of others.

When Jesus said, "Pray like this," He meant those words in the context of deep relationship with the Father—the Father who is worthy, otherworldly, almighty, pure, and loving. As we pray for people who hurt us, we must settle into God's worthiness in the midst of that pain. We do that by worshiping, taking the focus off our circumstances, and choosing to look heavenward to say and sing and write things about our impossible God.

It's a sheer act of will, this worship. Many of our painful relationships could be put to right, at least in the way we frame them, if we spent more time shouting about God's goodness than yelling at or about the people who hurt us. As we evaluate the difficult people in our lives in the midst of worship, we will be able to see them as gifts.

Begin with the Gift

ON A RECENT RUN, I SPRINTED (WELL, JOGGED) PAST A FULLY LEAFED Bradford pear tree, its white blossoms spent. The tree boasted several brown leaves still clinging to its branches, even as the new green preened. I wondered how those ugly dead leaves would give up their hold on the tree. In the crux of that thought, the wind picked up. The brown leaves let go of their geriatric grip and fluttered to the ground. Had the wind calmed, the only other way to strip the decay from the green would be for a person to stand on tiptoe and pull off the spent foliage.

It's the same in our lives. God sends winds (trials) our way to blow away the chaff in our lives. But He also sends people to pluck what is atrophying in our hearts. Both the wind and the people are gifts. We must start with that mind-set.

That person who is perplexing you? A gift. The friend who says hard things? A gift. The family member who spreads rumors about you? A gift. The ministry person who vies for power? A gift.

In the midst of one of the most trying times in my marriage, God called me to something very strange. A friend had hurt several people through her actions. Because of her anger, I had no desire to intervene; but God made it clear that I was to say something to her.

So I did.

And the situation between us crashed and burned.

I didn't confront beautifully. And she didn't respond well.

In the midst of this season, I consulted with a mentor, a wise woman who understood the situation. I wanted more than anything to make Jesus smile, to do the right thing. As I poured out my fear story, the mentor stopped me, stunning me with her words. "This is not about your friend," she told me. "God is doing something in you, something beautiful."

Her words reoriented me. Although I'd felt compelled to talk to my friend, inevitably God would use this difficult person to change me. And He did. In the fallout of that confrontation, I learned how to rely on God for my strength. I had to practice the discipline of letting God defend my reputation. I learned that relationships are fragile and that sometimes things change quickly between people. I learned the painful art of moving on. I felt a kinship to Jesus as I did what I felt was the right thing, even when others pushed against it. And I found joy in obeying Jesus despite a painful outcome.

The icing on the relational cake came when this experience evaporated a distance I felt in my marriage. I had no earthly idea that simple obedience to confront a friend would result in marital rejuvenation. Which goes to show that the most important thing we can do to help our relationships is to obey God in whatever He asks us. I won't run around counseling others to confront their friends to save their marriages. But I will say there is power in obedience. And when we have difficult relationships, God often uses them as gifts in our lives—to shape us, conform us to His Son, and make us gutsier and stronger.

I could give multiple examples in my life. I'm sure you could too. Every single person on this earth is a gift from God. He created each of us. Sure, we may be ragged or scared or angry, but we are all image bearers of an amazing

God. Because of that, we all have worth. Even those people who connive to hurt you, who choose to inflict wounds, are image bearers.

It's difficult to see people who injure us as gifts, but it's necessary if we're going to live open lives. Seeing my past, particularly the relationships there, as a gift has been the linchpin to the greatest healing in my life. I can be like Joseph, who said, "You intended to harm me, but God intended it for good to accomplish what is now being done, the saving of many lives" (Gen. 50:20 NIV). Because of the sexual abuse, I now can offer hope to those who have suffered it. Because of parental neglect, I can spot a kid in an abusive home and offer empathy. Because of the sexually charged nature of my home growing up, I can clearly discern the evil of pornography and run the other way. Because of fathers moving in and out of my life, I have the deepest, most significant commitment to my heavenly Father. Because of deprivation and loneliness, I've learned to find healthy relationships with my family, and I've found joy in letting Jesus fill the empty places.

Simply put, I would not be the Christ follower I am today without the painful people from my past. They were and are gifts. Messy, problematic gifts, but gifts nonetheless. Romans 8:28 is entirely true. God does cause every single thing in our lives, even relational trial, to bring about a better result. We only need to trust Him, be patient, welcome difficult people as gifts, and anticipate with joy what God will do.

Begin with an Open Heart

WE DON'T NEED TO BE PUSHOVERS TO PRAY LIKE THIS. WE DON'T NEED TO BE abuse victims either. No, we need to be strong, yet sweet—thick-skinned, yet tenderhearted. It means we cultivate open hearts to Jesus and the people He populates our lives with. To be open is to be anticipatory. It's to have *levav-shalem*, a Hebrew term that means "complete heart."[4] In order to have complete hearts, we must begin from a place of healing and abundance. I heard a story that illustrates what I mean.

Sara, a kindergartner, told her mom that she looked forward to Valentine's Day. Her teacher had helped each student create a mailbox from a tissue container. "I decorated my box with glitter and hearts and cupids," she said.

"That's beautiful," her mom said.

"I want to make my valentines now." Sara grabbed the craft box and spread out her supplies on the table.

Her mom provided paper lace doilies and fancy scissors. But inside, her mom cringed. She knew Sara had experienced a lot of teasing and hazing at school. Sara wasn't like the other kids. Sara stood out but not in a good way. She knew, too, that most kids purchased their valentines. "Don't you want to head to the store where we can buy some cards?" her mom asked.

"No," she said. "I want to make them. One for each friend in my class."

Her mom sank deeper inside herself, wanting desperately to rescue Sara from homemade valentines and the ridicule that might ensue. But Sara was determined, so she waited as Sara painstakingly glued hearts and glitter and doilies on cards.

Sara's mom prayed that day something fierce. She ached, knowing the inevitability of her daughter's heart breaking once again.

But when Sara came home, she skipped. A smile brightened her face.

"Did you get a lot of valentines?" her mom asked.

"No, just one. From my teacher," Sara said.

Her mom let out a long breath, weariness and sadness settling in. "Oh."

"Mom, guess what?" Sara giggled and danced in a circle.

"What?" What could possibly make her daughter so happy?

"I made twenty-eight valentines, and there were exactly twenty-eight kids in my class! I had just enough for everyone!" Sara laughed and smiled.

Sara's mom thanked Jesus for a daughter who'd been far more concerned about making enough for the bullies in her class than about whether the bullies would reciprocate.

And that's how Jesus wants us to be with life. I'm afraid I'm far too concerned that people are going to do right by me, that they will fill and exceed my expectations. I've focused so much on my needs that I've become entombed in my heart. The more and more pain that friends heap my way, the more I isolate and close up my life.

But we serve a giving God who gives us everything we

need. From that abundance, our main concern is that we'll have enough valentines for the people whom God puts in our class. Then with this full and openhearted way of life, we will rejoice when we have the opportunity to hand out another valentine.

God's heart for us is that we live like Sara, not hiding away in our pain, but bringing that pain to Him to solve. It's not that we live in denial either. We let God know what bothers us, who hurts us, and how we really want to close off our hearts. We learn the art of being honest with the Almighty, of laying our pain at the feet of the One who embodied Sara's heart. He gave it all, even when the bullies shouted accusations His way. He gave a valentine to every last person on earth—just enough—so we could experience His homemade salvation.

"PRAY LIKE THIS" IS AN INVITATION FROM JESUS TO TAKE YOUR DIFficult relationships and place them in His hands. It's a beckoning to give He-who-understands every violation, every terrible memory, every regret. It's to settle that God is God and we are not. As we begin this adventure of healing in the aftermath of people's abuse or neglect or terrible words spoken, remember to begin with Jesus, the One who receives our anguish and empathizes. And because He has, by His grace, so will we.

QUESTIONS FOR GROWTH

- What's your first reaction when someone hurts you? How can choosing to pray help you transform your reaction?
- What role has worship played in your difficult friendships? How might choosing to worship help you cope with further pain?
- How does seeing relational pain as kinship with Jesus help you frame the way you see it? How has Jesus helped you navigate pain in the past week?
- Looking back on painful relationships, how have they become gifts to you? When is it hard to see them that way?
- How did the story of Sara and the valentines help you understand the importance of living an openhearted life? How are you like Sara?

“Our Father in Heaven”

Live in Your Father’s Affection

“OUR FATHER IN HEAVEN”—FOUR SIMPLE WORDS—YET LACED WITH meaning. The first words of this famous prayer show intimacy, an expression of closeness—not with a distant, angry deity but with a God who is called Father, the kind of relationship everyone longs for. But His words continue with “in heaven.” With that phrase, Jesus reminded us of God’s location, where He sits enthroned far above, seated in heavenly realms. God is as near as our breath and as far as our imagination. As we wrangle our way through a difficult relationship, as we languish in the land of regret and injury, we have a way up. We have prayer—a treasure we direct to God, who sits as King over the universe.

The framework of this chapter is simple. I’ve divided it into three parts.

Our.

Father.

In heaven.

"Our" because we need to understand the community aspect of this prayer. "Father" because many of us struggle with our earthly fathers and equating God to them. And "in heaven" to remind us of God's loftiness.

Our

THE SCRIPTURE DOESN'T SAY, "*MY* FATHER IN HEAVEN." IT USES "our." There are no singular pronouns in the entire prayer. This prayer should be prayed with relationships in mind, which makes it a great foundational prayer for those of us dealing with the aftermath of someone's thoughtlessness. We pray for our hearts, our worries, our injuries, and our need to forgive. We pray for the others the person has hurt. And we pray for the person who injured us, that the person would find joy in Jesus, that reconciliation could bud in the tangle of pain.

Though it's not always intuitive, when we pray in the context of community for the welfare of those who have hurt us, we experience the surprising blessing of God. Even Job, whose "helpful" friends skewered him with their words, found prosperity of soul after he prayed for his friends: "The LORD restored the fortunes of Job, when he had prayed for his friends. And the LORD gave Job twice as much as he had before" (Job 42:10 ESV).

A chapter before Jesus uttered the Lord's Prayer, He reminded His followers of the importance of loving those who bother, hate, or abuse us. We reflect our love for Him in the way we love the "ours" in our lives. Jesus said,

> You have heard the law that says, "Love your neighbor" and hate your enemy. But I say, love your enemies! Pray for those who persecute you! In that way, you will be acting as true children of your Father in heaven. For he gives his sunlight to both the evil and the good, and he sends rain on the just and the unjust alike. If you love only those who love you, what reward is there for that? Even corrupt tax collectors do that much. If you are kind only to your friends, how are you different from anyone else? Even pagans do that. But you are to be perfect, even as your Father in heaven is perfect. (Matt. 5:43–48)

When we begin to grasp the communal aspect of this prayer, we see again that God intended us to be in relationship, to relate to those around us. He asks us to become as He is—a community. God always existed in relationship in trinitarian form: God the Father, God the Son, God the Holy Spirit. All three in holy symbiosis. All three connected. All three loving the others. His creation of humankind derived from a joyful expression of what He already experienced in relationship. It's no wonder that after God created Adam and saw that he was alone and needy, He created Eve to walk alongside the man. He started this world as a relationship, and the first people He created, He created for relationship.

This is why living in the free fall of someone's sin hurts so much. We know way down deep that God intends harmony, community, and joy in each other's presence. And because we know this, we take risks in relationships even though it's hard. We share our hearts. And when we connect, we find that kind of rapturous joy God experiences in Himself, a foretaste of what kind of joy we'll experience in heaven.

Then sin enters the picture, just as it did in the garden, and with sin, discord. The pain we feel runs deeper than we expect. It slays hope, trashes our resolve. It emaciates us, embitters our hearts, and shuts us down. Why? Because we hold heaven in our hearts as image bearers of God. We want harmony. We long for relationships the way God intended.

We tend to live in an either-or world, a starkly black-and-white one where it's easier for us to see the sin in others (because it hurts us so much) than it is for us to see the sin in ourselves. Since everyone in the world struggles with this issue, we walk this earth with megachips on our shoulders, believing ourselves to be victims of everyone else's selfishness.

But the biblical truth is we all sin. We all contribute to the ripping apart of the community. Other people live in the fallout of our bad treatment of them. We're all in this heartache together.

Since God is our Father, He grieves when He watches us hurt each other. If you're a parent, you understand this. When I see my kids bicker and hurt each other, I ache too. I long for their reconciliation, and I pray they'll learn the art of humility and forgiveness. God relates to the entire world the same way. As the Father of us all, God watches us fight and tear into each other—no matter how justified both parties feel—and aches for our reconciliation.

But community does not always represent heartache. God uses people to heal us, to be agents of reconciliation. Finding true community can be amazing.

Recently I experienced the positive aspect of community even as I grieved broken relationships. I read the words of a grandmother after she found out her granddaughter got engaged. She wrote she'd been praying for her granddaughter's future spouse since she was in the womb. I teared up.

> I sent an e-mail to my friend D'Ann: Most days I'm totally fine not having family support. But today it feels hard. It's very, very hard not having parents who support you, who pray for you, who give you godly wisdom. It's hard not to have grandparents who do the same. There are times I feel orphaned in that aspect. There's such a huge void.

D'Ann answered with these sweet words:

> And yet isn't God big enough to fill that void? Doesn't He declare Himself a father to the fatherless (and a mother to the motherless)? You will be that mother and grandmother for your children, but it all has to start

> somewhere. Think of those children of Israel whose parents were so unfaithful God had to kill them off. Then He took their children into the Promised Land to fight the enemies with no parental support and a bad parental history. They didn't even have Moses. They only had the Lord, and He wanted them to trust that that was enough.

She continued,

> Just because a grandmother prays doesn't mean it will all be hunky-dory. Just because there isn't a grandmother who prays doesn't mean it won't be. Don't believe the lies! God is enough. He has always been and always will be enough. And He has given you and Patrick tons and tons of surrogate family to be to you and your children exactly what you need. Blood relation doesn't make things more valid. If it did, adoption would be pointless. I've seen you make such progress lately. Tell Satan that the Lord is a better mother and father to you than anyone else would ever be.

In my sadness over my family of origin, D'Ann reminded me of others who are my family, of God who fills the deepest void. That's the power of community to change our lives, offer healing, and help us move forward. Unfortunately after we've been hurt, we revert to catastrophic thinking, making everyone an enemy, believing the worst about every single person. We cut ourselves off, protecting our hearts, thinking this will keep us safe. But when we do, we shortchange the healing process.

Truth: God uses the thing that crushes us to heal us. If we've been injured in community, He uses community to heal us. That's not to say we run headlong into toxic relationships. We are to grow up and learn discernment from our negative experiences. It means God leads us toward healthy community to help us recover from difficult community. It means we risk again for the sake of our healing, even though that seems entirely counterintuitive.

God is *our* Father. All of us together. When we realize that He loves every single person on this earth with enormous affection, we see how small our love is, and we begin to understand that we're more like God when we're forgiving those who sin against us. We're more like Him when we gather community to ourselves rather than shun it.

Father

GOD IS OUR FATHER. AND AS HIS CHILDREN, WE MUST CULTIVATE AN accurate view of God's father heart. *Father,* as a name for God, appears only rarely in the Old Testament, and it always occurs in reference to God fathering the nation of Israel, not a one-on-one intimate relationship between the individual believer and God. But that changes in the New Testament.

The Greek word in the Lord's Prayer is *pater,* which usually refers to a man who has fathered a child (it is also used metaphorically, as a father in the church). And Jesus uses a form of *pater* ten times in Matthew 6:1–8 alone, speaking not only of his relationship to the Father, but also referring to God as the believer's heavenly Father. This word then occurs more than forty times in the Gospels and throughout the New Testament.[1] Clearly by inviting us to call God *Father,* Jesus began a revolution in understanding who God is. No longer the far-off deity who deals in nations and world conflict, God becomes as close to us as a parent—the best possible parent.

Three chapters before the Lord's Prayer, the Pharisees and Sadducees referred to Abraham as their father. Dallas Seminary professor Sandra Glahn reveals just how shocking it might have been to the disciples to hear God referred to as Father: "Up to this point, God's people recognized Abraham as their father. They worshipped God as the Creator and Lord but never as 'our Father.' Today we're so familiar with the teaching about God as heavenly Father that we lack the understanding the disciples had of awe, reverence, and holy fear."[2]

Jesus referred to God as His Father more than fifty times in the New Testament. He called Him no other name, which is astounding if you think about it. Always Daddy. Always Papa. Always Father. Always Dad.[3] He gave us an example to follow and taught we aren't children by chance. The God of the universe, who spun worlds into existence, chose us, adopted us. We've been reconciled to a right relationship with our Father through Jesus' sacrifice on the cross, a task He struggled with: "He said, 'Abba, Father, all things are possible for you. Remove this cup from me. Yet not what I will, but what you will'" (Mark 14:36 ESV). Because of His gritty obedience, His beautiful relationship to the Father, we have the privilege of calling God "Daddy."

Paul further emphasized this tender nature of Father (*Abba*, an Aramaic word, basically means "Papa" or "Daddy" in our vernacular)[4] when he referred to this grand adoption: "For you did not receive the spirit of slavery to fall back into fear, but you have received the Spirit of adoption as sons, by whom we cry, 'Abba! Father!'" (Rom. 8:15 ESV). He reiterated in Galatians 4:6 (ESV), "And because you are sons, God has sent the Spirit of his Son into our hearts, crying, 'Abba! Father!'" In his sermon about this section of Scripture, Charles Spurgeon wrote, "If I be his child, then I have a portion in his heart here, and I shall have a portion in his house above."[5]

With this grand adoption as the backdrop, for those who are Christ followers, we see no orphans in the kingdom of God. I may be a fatherless girl with a daddy need the size of Texas, but it's not true that I'm an orphan. The God of the universe saw fit to choose me, a waif of a girl bent on her destruction, for His own. He healed me, gave me hope, and set my feet on the firm foundation of His love.

Here's the problem though. Many of us have earthly fathers who have hurt us. We assign God traits that our fathers possessed, and that assignment distorts our view of Him.

My father and the way he lived his life provided plenty of distortion. I've tried to write a book about the enigma that is my father but haven't been able to do it. Too much darkness. Too many questions. A lot of confusion.

I called him Jim. Not Dad. Not Father. Not Daddy. Just his first name. It created a distance, one that had to be there because of the divorce and the nature of our visits every other Sunday. He swooped into my life on those days, exposing me to his world—a mosaic of art, nature, photography, food, and eclectic festivals. He wrote me poetry. Before self-publishing was even a thought, he purchased handmade blank books and filled them with stories, pictures, and poems about me. He made me the heroine of the stories. I knew he loved me.

So when my mother sat in her small Datsun that December morning after pulling me from class, I could taste the anxiety there. "Your father is dead," she told me.

A child of three divorces by then, I asked, "Which one?"

"Jim."

"Oh." I don't remember crying. I don't remember reacting. But deep inside, my center careened off-kilter. Jim, who loved me, died. At ten years old, I wondered, *Will anyone ever love me again? Will I ever be special to another grown-up?* When forced to join the fatherless club, I started down the path of rediscovering this truth year after year: a child never outgrows her need for a father. Even today I sense the vacuum. My father missed my life—graduating valedictorian of my high school, following in his literary footsteps with an English degree. He didn't walk me down the aisle. He didn't hear the yelp of my first, second, or third child. He didn't cheer for me as I followed in his footsteps as a writer. He never held one of my books.

In reading this, you may see a sense of nostalgia as I look back on his life. But I've left things out of the story. I mourned a hero for many, many years, believing my life less-than because of his passing. But now I've come to see it was God's severe but beautiful mercy on my life that my father died when he did.

Now that I'm a parent, I realize that good fathers don't tell their children about sex when they're too young to understand. They don't ask their daughters to bathe them. They don't take nude pictures of their daughters, develop them, then show them to others. They don't take pictures of naked women in awkward positions and show them to their daughters. That was my father too.

A wild genius of a man. A writer. A poet. A photographer. A father. A husband twice. A lover of words. But a consumer of sexual perversion, who seemed to be grooming his daughter.

So when I read, "Our Father in heaven," I stumble over the words. I'm still living in the effects of my father's deviance. How can I possibly view God as good, God as regenerative, or God as nurturer? When I think of my father, I think of awful pictures that I can't erase from my mind forty years later. I think of nudity. I think of the perverse words he wrote. I think of a genius obsessed with sexual addiction.

If I can't trust my father to love me well, to nurture and soothe me, how can I trust my heavenly Father? The next thought careens into my heart: if I can't trust God, I can't trust anyone. This spills over into my relationships with every person I meet. And it stifles my ability to love others. If I live with a deep suspicion, always cynical about others and their intentions, how can I truly love others?

This is why having a proper view of God helps our relationships. That undergirding trust informs our ability to embrace others.

Although I once mourned a hero's death in my father, I still stumble over the reality of his life. If we stay in that place of conundrum, we'll walk wounded, pushing others away. We need to settle these issues now so we can live fully alive, joyful.

You may not face the same perplexity when you think about your earthly father, but the truth is, no earthly father is perfect. And some are downright ungodly. So many of us haul baggage with us when we say the word *father.* It conjures up memories, broken promises, regret, shame, fear. How can we deal rightly with conflict and relational discord when we can't approach the fatherhood of God in a truthful manner?

As I look at this inauguration of the Lord's Prayer, I grapple with five truths, not in progression but in a tangle of emotions and theology. Somehow this foundation, these words, stir waters I'd rather not roil. As one who has shoved the memory of an enigmatic father way down deep, it's not intuitive to go there. But I must. And so must you. This is for anyone who has allowed a negative view of a parent to color God in a bad light, then frame every other relationship in that light.

Truth One

We know when something isn't quite right in our earthly relationships. This knowing beautifully shows God's standard of perfection. So our earthly parents' neglect or foibles or self-centeredness points us to the One who personifies attentiveness, faultlessness, and sacrificial love.

Truth Two

The longing in us for a great relationship with a parent reveals a universal desire. If we've had a difficult relationship with a parent, instead of seeing this as a way to blame God, we can instead channel that energy to pursuing God, who ultimately fills our deepest yearnings. His perfect parenthood becomes the place we rest our weary, sin-tired hearts.

Truth Three

One parent's sin doesn't trump God's goodness. It is hard, though, to see this. Our initial instinct is to blame God for giving us the parents He did. We struggle to see them as gifts, as parts of a sovereign plan to bring us to Himself. In my life, I've seen how my childhood and my problematic relationship with my parents actually opened up an avenue for me to meet Jesus. I don't know whether I would've possessed that longing if I'd not experienced what I had. And when I experienced God's goodness for the first time, the abuse from the past faded a bit in light of it.

Truth Four

We shouldn't universalize our experience of one bad relationship, nor should we project it onto God. To protect our hearts, we make sweeping statements about every person, and even God, based on one negative experience. And then we avoid. God is completely other, unlike us in every possible way. When we project what people do onto Him, we judge God.

Truth Five

Satan wants nothing more than for us to run from God's goodness because of someone else's bad behavior. In fact, this seems to be his favorite scheme. I meet more people who've fallen away from Christ because a Christian has hurt them, particularly a Christian leader, which includes Christian parents. Blaming God for someone else's bad behavior and disengaging from Him and from life usher in isolation, anger, distance, and that high wall around our hearts. And when we live behind that wall, our hearts grow cold, bitter, and unwieldy.

In Heaven

PLACING HEAVEN AT THE GENESIS OF THIS PRAYER REMINDS US THAT while God is our affectionate Father, He is also God, filling the entire universe, living regally in heaven where His throne exists. While we struggle on earth where relationships ignite, inflame, then burn out, we can rest in knowing the eternality of God. While our friendships give way to entropy, from order to disorder, there is a realm of order and peace.

Heaven can help us when we fret about others. When we think of heaven, we think of a spiritual realm. This reminds us that our prayers, eternally important and potent, are spiritual—yet heard.

Heaven looms lofty above the earth. So our hearts must reflect this, revering God, hollering His fame, not our own.

Heaven is a perfect place, so when we pray, we must remember that Jesus made us whole. He cleansed our hearts and hands, both lifted heavenward. And someday, in light of heaven, our difficult relationships will be made right.

Heaven is expansive, which reminds us of the expansiveness of God. He is bigger than the discord we bring to Him. He is more immense than all the relational difficulties of every person in the world combined. Because He is in heaven, He rules over all. This kingship reminds us of His kingdom, and as we pray, we pray for His kingdom. (We'll address this later in chapter 4.)

We live in the great tension of earth and heaven, the now and the not yet, the familiar and the far away. God's nearness and His otherness become a beautiful dichotomy. He is near, yet revered. Heaven reminds us that we taste and glimpse peace now, but that someday we'll fully experience it. The lion and the lamb will hang out together. That enemy we battle has the heavenly potential to become an ally.

"Our Father in Heaven"

TODAY AS I PRAY THAT PRAYER, JUST THOSE FOUR SIMPLE WORDS, I'm facing a relational battle where I have hurt friends. In a few minutes I will talk to them, apologize, and ask for grace.

My stomach knots, and I repeat, "Our Father in heaven." I remind myself that God put us all together on this planet as an "us" and that each one has a responsibility to the other. And as I fail relationally, I fall on the mercy of my Abba Father, who has chosen to adopt me, who sent His Son to die for my sins as He walked this earth in the midst of troublesome relationships. He is my Daddy, yet He understands. In heaven He looks down upon this situation, the one I dread, with eyes of wisdom, a heart of grace, and an affectionate desire for reconciliation.

"Our Father in heaven," I pray again as I reach for the phone.

QUESTIONS FOR GROWTH

- How has community broken you? How has it healed you?
- Why does Jesus want us to hang out with others, particularly when people hurt us? Why does He think community is important?
- How does your view of your earthly father color the way you see your heavenly Father? Positively? Negatively?
- Mary wrote, “If I can’t trust God, I can’t trust anyone.” Have you ever experienced this thinking? When? Why? How does your trust of God spill over into your relationships?
- When relationships are hard, how does thinking of heaven help you cope with them now? What about heaven appeals to you? Scares you?

"May Your Name Be Kept Holy"

Allow God to Be God

WHEN YOU'RE CLOSE TO DEATH, YOU TEND TO SEE YOUR LIFE FLASH on the movie theater of your mind. Which I did. But I also saw Jesus.

Not in a He-is-standing-right-there way but in a majestic way.

I flew from South Africa to Washington, DC, after Cape Town 2010, a humbling, invigorating conference. It proved to be a once-in-a-lifetime event with leaders from nearly every country talking about world missions. I heard many languages, had life-altering conversations, and watched God answer a very specific prayer.

I'd wanted to meet a persecuted Christian, someone who

had suffered for Jesus. And God brought to my table group an Iraqi man who had been imprisoned and threatened. Still, he dared to operate a radio station where he prayed for people on the air. After we talked, I instantly wanted him to become my father.

Another person at my little table needed to hear my story of redemption, namely, the hope that God provides after sexual abuse. She confided in me about her abusive father, how she needed to escape his grip.

A man from South Africa changed my life when he looked me in the eyes, hands on either side of my shoulders, and said, "Mary, I apologize on behalf of men—all men—and what they did to you." He wept. I wept. And a hole in my heart started to close up.

Another man shared his dream of writing and gave me his book on the great hymns of the faith. A woman I'd not previously met toured me around South Africa, igniting a friendship that continues today. During the sessions, I cried so much I blew my nose ring clear out, and I experienced the holy hush that comes only when revival whispers your name. I left South Africa changed, in awe of the relationships God brought my way, and thankful for all the lessons I'd learned.

Our plane stopped in Dakar to refuel before its long flight across the Atlantic in the dead of night. The man next to me had also attended the conference, so we talked about our experiences and our lives back home. Then we drifted off to sleep.

In one violent drop, at 2:00 a.m. our plane free-fell probably a thousand feet. Personal items flew about the cabin. People screamed. I felt the sting of my seat belt holding me back in my chair. Without thinking, I grabbed my new friend's knee, then quickly retreated, saying, "I'm sorry," about five times.

"That's okay," he said. And I heard fear in his voice—this from a man who had traveled the world.

The next moment, the plane's nose pointed oceanward. We angled toward the earth. For several seconds.

I knew I would die.

I prayed.

I saw my life flash.

Then Jesus.

Not in a vision. Just a knowing. I breathed deeply and realized that in this last moment of life, I needed Him—Him alone. My heart that had rattled and skipped in the noseward dive instantly felt peace.

The plane jerked its way to blessed horizontal. The pilot said nothing, never did tell us what happened.

Life Is Fragile

THE HOLINESS OF GOD, HIS POWER, HIS OTHERNESS PERMEATED ME in that moment. I realized just how fragile life was, how easily a plane could slip from its air pocket and plummet to earth. I saw brevity and my smallness, just a little pale dot on a big green-and-blue planet. I thought on the enormity of God, who watches every airplane flight, who cares about each person aboard, who gathers people in South Africa, who creates every single thing every soul can see and touch and smell and breathe in.

I hushed in that holy moment, settled my heart before Him, and once again gave Him my life.

That's the essence of "may your name be kept holy"—an upward focus that sets the tone for the rest of the petition. We remember repeating "hallowed be thy name" but don't quite understand. The English word *hallowed* in the Greek is *hagiastheto*. It means "to see as or make holy, set apart."[1] It nears inapproachability, meaning God's holiness is so above us that we can barely touch, understand, or grapple with it. The Greek word translated "name" is *onoma,* and it connotes more than just a name.[2] It means the essence or nature of the person attached to the name. In ancient societies, names equaled the people behind them. So when we revere God's name, we elevate Him to extreme heights. We shout His ability. Cyprian, a third-century bishop, said that the Father is hallowed "not that we wish for God that He be hallowed by our prayers, but because we seek from the Lord that His name be hallowed in us."[3]

I had a holy ache after the plane dropped from the sky. In the aftermath of that nosedive, I wanted God's name and character to be magnified by the way I lived my life. That can sound so ethereal and aspirational, so detached from day-to-day living. It echoes platitudes. But I meant it. And I mean it now as I type these words. In the past few years, I've learned that the way I live out the words I say has everything to do with how I interact with the people in my life. How do we make God's name holy in our relationships? How does hallowing God make us love our neighbor better?

We Can't Love God, Yet Hate His People

SOME OF US ARE UNDER THE IMPRESSION THAT WE CAN LOVE GOD but hate His church. We say, "May Your name be great," while gossiping about our friend's reputation and still believe everything is okay. It's not.

The two commandments (love God, love others: Matt. 22:36–40) hold hands and cannot be separated. Why? This verse makes it painfully simple: "Whoever claims to love God yet hates a brother or sister is a liar. For whoever does not love their brother and sister, whom they have seen, cannot love God, whom they have not seen" (1 John 4:20 NIV). You cannot love God and hate people. You cannot revere Him, yet dismiss the people He made. If you say you love God, yet skirt away from others in isolation, you are a liar.

Not easy words to write or hear or read. A liar is someone who says untrue words. A deceiver. So when we hate people who have wronged us, yet hallow God's name in church, we are liars.

One author puts it bluntly: "To think that we are entitled to love God and hate his people is sin. And, perhaps as important, it is impossible. Frankly, when we think we are loving

Jesus but hating his people, we are actually loving Jesus so little that his people don't matter anymore."[4] Because people matter to God. He created us, and He has poured Himself into us if we call ourselves Christ followers. His Holy Spirit resides within, giving us the will to love those who feel unlovely to us. When we refuse to love others, we quench the Holy Spirit and hog-tie His ability to live and move in love through us.

Growing Pains

THIS IS WHY WE HAVE A GROWTH PROBLEM IN THE CHURCH. WE SAY one thing, then act another way, leaving God's love out of the picture. We say we love God, but when someone wrongs us, we usurp His position, take on His name, and place ourselves in the judge's seat. We declare our enemy unfit for our forgiveness. And then we spend our lifetimes walling off our hearts, isolating ourselves from others, and embittering ourselves. Doing this is the opposite of revering God's name.

If we revere His name, we dare to take relational risks. If we herald His power, we trust it enough to say, "I'm sorry," or "I forgive you." If we worship God's holiness, we shudder under His immensity and dare to make things right with others. If we love Jesus, we live as He did—engaging the very people who would crucify Him later. If we adore our Father, we give Him our bitterness, take the healing path He offers, and search for ways to reach out to others, even in our pain. If we love to make God's name famous, we refrain from talk that denigrates others. If we revel in the God who made all of us, we don't demonize people who differ from us. (Consider that every single person on this earth differs from God in every way, yet He loves us.) If we praise God for all the amazing things He has done in our lives, we will strain to see His handiwork in our enemies' lives.

Loving others isn't easy. And at times I don't love well. I'd rather trumpet everyone else's failures and barbs and minimize my own. I'd rather God forgive my mountain of sins than choose to forgive the molehill of sins that others have perpetrated against me. I'd rather bask in my self-righteous rightness than consider that I may be the perpetrator in need of others' grace and forgiveness.

After that airplane ride, I had a holy hush in my soul, but it wasn't easy for me to transform that hush into positive action in my relationships. As soon as I came home, we faced a relational trial with friends of several years. Through excruciating conversations, we eventually parted ways. Although I do believe God parts us from others (and not all relationships are meant to last a lifetime), we experienced bewildering hurt. I didn't always honor God through that disappointment. At times, I gossiped. At other times, I nursed bitterness. It is still hard for me to forgive. But recently God gave me insight into the situation that better helped me see it from His perspective.

God's Way to Approach Difficult Relationships

WHAT CAN WE DO TO REVERE GOD IN THE WAY WE HANDLE OUR DIFficult relationships?

Stop Rehashing the Past

We do not revere the name and otherness of God when we continually remind ourselves of the pain we experienced. When we rehash, we rehearse, then relive the pain, which ends up poisoning us further. Have you ever met someone who couldn't let go of an offense? Do you want to be like that? Author Stephen Mansfield pens a warning to us: "You've been playing your bitter story over and over again in your mind. As you do, you keep hardening your feelings and deepening the wound each time you relive the jagged facts. Now, you can do this for the rest of your life if you want. But play it out. What will you be in a decade or two or three?"[5]

Self-help gurus have reminded us to live life in light of the legacy we leave behind. Project yourself into the future. If you keep holding on to this offense, what kind of person will you be? Do you want to be that person? And how does a bitter, closed-off, angry person represent God well? How does that revere or praise Him? How does that reveal His nature to the world?

Yes, it happened.

Yes, it was entirely unfair.

Yes, it hurt.

Yes, you want vengeance.

But it's time to let go. Vent your frustration full bent to the heavens. Shout if you must. Holler. Rant. Stomp your feet. But then relinquish. Hand over your anger and pain to the One who knows how to take them. That is a holy act, and it shows God you're more interested in being like

Him—forgiving, joy filled, free—than becoming an enemy to others.

The loss of one of my friends still torments me. In the halcyon days of our early friendship, we formed an instant bond. As we grew closer, I began to see some discrepancies in her life. I noticed that people were either her close friends or her bitter enemies, worthy of scorn and disdain. This worked as long as I was in the former group. But as I got brave enough to talk to her about this issue, she recoiled, lashed out, and placed me in the second category.

For a long time, I felt the betrayal down deep. I processed this with two close friends who knew my either-love-you-or-hate-you friend. They encouraged me to stop rehashing. But I persisted. Why had she turned on me? What did I do wrong? I did recognize how I hurt her, so I took time to apologize and ask forgiveness, only to be misunderstood. At that point I knew it was time to let go.

Over several years, I came in contact with people who experienced the same turning tendencies with my friend. After realizing this friend had recoiled on many other people, I knew I'd been right to let go of the friendship. Sometimes folks are irregular, and they have problems we cannot fix. There are people who are so injured from life that all they can do is lash out and blame everyone else for their problems. It does us no good to stay stuck, rehearsing the conversations.

I've learned the wisdom of the late gospel singer Keith Green. He sang, "Just do your best, and pray that it's blessed, and Jesus takes care of the rest."[6] Jesus calls us to that kind of trust. We search our hearts, apologize for what we can, then move on, trusting God to pick up the pieces. Rehearsing and rehashing only stick us in the mud, keep us injured and hurt, and prevent us from the forward momentum God wants for our lives.

To get beyond the pain of a relationship, we must acknowledge the pain first so we can move on later. This is part of learning the art of grieving—and embracing lament for a time.

Lament When You're Hurt

When we're hurt, we tend to retreat, nurse wounds, or lash out—any number of unhealthy reactions. What would happen if we trained ourselves to turn to God in praise instead? The Lament Psalms offer encouragement in these kinds of situations. They start with a rant and end in praise. It's a great road map for us in our hurt and helps us revere God even when we're bewildered.

Lament Psalms typically follow this pattern:

1. Talk directly to God as an introduction, and state your case.
2. Detail the problem; hold nothing back. (Sometimes this is done repeatedly throughout the psalm.)
3. Pray, and ask for His specific help.
4. Confess your trust to God, even though it's hard.
5. Praise God for all He's done and will do.

Take note of this pattern in Psalm 13 (ESV). My comments are enclosed in brackets.

To the choirmaster: A Psalm of David.

[Talk directly to God as an introduction, and state
your case.]
How long, O Lord? Will you forget me forever?
How long will you hide your face from me?
[Detail the problem; hold nothing back.]
How long must I take counsel in my soul
and have sorrow in my heart all the day?
How long shall my enemy be exalted over me?

[Pray, and ask for His specific help.]
Consider and answer me, O Lord my God;
light up my eyes, lest I sleep the sleep of death,
lest my enemy say, "I have prevailed over him,"
lest my foes rejoice because I am shaken.

[Confess your trust to God, even though it's hard.]
But I have trusted in your steadfast love;
my heart shall rejoice in your salvation.
[Praise God for all He's done and will do.]
I will sing to the Lord,
because he has dealt bountifully with me.

Spend some time after you've been hurt to write your own Lament Psalm. As I mentioned in my book *You Can Raise Courageous and Confident Kids,* our family wrote Lament Psalms when we moved overseas. Not only did that give us a greater insight into our kids' struggles, but they also got to see how we wrestled with living in a foreign country, facing loneliness and difficult relationships.

Are you facing a relational struggle now? Take a moment to write out your lament. Give yourself permission to say it all, to be raw and honest. You're not going to surprise God. He knows all this anyway. It'll be a way to experience catharsis and a pathway toward praise. Because ultimately if you've spent yourself on the page, you have a better ability to turn heavenward in praise.

It may seem counterintuitive to praise God after someone has hurt you. But the process of lamenting helps turn the corner from angst to alleluia.

Here is a lament I wrote just now about a difficult relationship I've walked through:

Dear Jesus, thank You for hearing me, for seeing me.

I'm having a hard time loving my friends,
Distracted by their blindness,
Worried by the people they're hurting,
Wondering if I said enough.

I know You say that we're to be faithful in small things,
So I get discouraged when I see people unfaithful in things big and small,
And they don't seem to care a whit about it.
It makes me tired.
But You know all that.

In fact, You know the situation much better than I do.
You see clearly.
While I see dimly.
I choose to believe that You are bigger than my friends,
That You are stronger than their sin,
That You are mightier than my bitterness,
That You are wiser than my puny assessment of the situation.

Lord Jesus, help me to see as You do.
Help me relinquish this friendship into Your hands.
Help me say the hard things when I'm supposed to,
Be quiet when You ask me to hush,
Have wisdom to step away if that's what You deem right,
To live without regret in terms of this relationship.

Please heal my heart in the aftermath.
Shine Your light on the dark parts of my heart
that want revenge.
Forgive me for my bitterness, my gossip, my fury.
I love You, Jesus.

Thank You for showing me what good relationships
should look like.
Help me be like You, a listener, an encourager, one
who speaks truth with love.
You are perfect and amazing and powerful and true.
And I love You for it.

Once and for all, I relinquish this friendship into
Your hands.
And I take my hands off it.
And I raise my hands to heaven to praise You.
Amen.

Don't let another day go by without letting out your laments to Jesus. He will use the process to set you free. Even as I typed the words, I felt a lightening, a sweetness. All is well, not because I wrote magical words but because God intersected my lament, revealed again that He is in control and turned me back toward the one thing that will set my heart right: praise.

If I've learned one thing on this earth, it's this: people who live in gratitude toward God have the most joyful lives.

Dare to be set free today by exercising that kind of praise. The roadblocks to growth and joy come when we forget the bigness of God and instead make people bigger than He is.

Don't Make People (or Their Opinions) Idols

Some of us believe that the fundamental point of life is for others to make us happy. I lived many, many years chasing after approval, love, and affirmation, hoping that one day I'd happen upon the magic formula for happiness. I believed it would involve all the people in my life loving me and singing my praises at precisely the same time.

But life doesn't work that way, particularly on the terra firma of earth. We're a bunch of sinful people tripping over each other, trying not to wound each other in the process (though some do make it a point to hurt). We're not a fine kettle of fish, swimming in harmony; we're a tank of piranhas devouring each other. That's reality.

Lifelong injury and bitterness come when we deify others, making them idols. What is an idol? It's something (someone) that you run to first when you need help. It's your first response. It's what you feel you need to be happy. An idol represents control. It's the ducks-in-a-row we long for on earth but seldom experience. It's anything (or anyone) in your life that is more important than God. Even good things can be idols, which makes identifying them very hard.

Making a person an idol is the opposite of revering God. How do you know whether you've made a person or people into idols?

- Your happiness is directly tied to the way someone treats you.
- If someone hurts you, your day/week/month is forever tainted.
- If someone is unavailable to you when you're hurting, you sink into devastation.
- Your friend or family member says to you, "Your expectations of me are too high. I can't live up to them."
- You fantasize about always being with someone.
- You believe your life will be complete only if a certain person would pay attention to you.
- You need someone's approval before you can attempt anything new.
- If one person disappoints you or goes a different way than you want him or her to, you ride on a constant roller coaster of prayer and then panic.
- Someone has the power to plunge you into either euphoria or depression.
- Your sin, sadness, or disappointment always hinges on some other person.

Parents can make idols of their children. Whether their children rebel or strive to live up to their high expectations, parents may tie their ultimate happiness to their kids' performance well into their adult years. Children can deify parents, under the shadow of their expectations, striving to meet an ideal that's not suited to their personalities. A spouse can make an idol of the other spouse, pouring all his or her needs into the spouse's basket, and when that spouse doesn't meet needs, he or she pouts, condemns, withdraws, or fights back to get his or her way. Friends can make other friends idols, hoping that one friendship will fill all the empty spots in their lives.

The truth? People will disappoint. They can't fill continually. Only Jesus can do that. Remember what He said to the woman at the well? Jesus told her, "Everyone who drinks this water will be thirsty again, but whoever drinks the water I give them will never thirst. Indeed, the water I give them will become in them a spring of water welling up to eternal life" (John 4:13–14 NIV). He is the only One who can give living water, the kind that fully satisfies. If we misplace our desires and look to people to fill us, we'll live angry lives, never quite filled up, blaming others for not doing their jobs.

Sometimes we wrap God in an idol cloak of others, reasoning that we're loving those people for God's sake or bowing to their needs to build God's glorious kingdom. We measure our identities by how well we love those people, how successful we feel when we nurture. Although it's not wrong to love people (obviously), it sneaks toward idolatry when our identities are tightly wound to the harmony of those relationships.

Conversely we endure abuse by those idols because we value their mistreatment more than we believe we're worthy of being treated well. We believe we deserve the abuse of others. In this broken state, we forget God's powerful story: We are loved; we are worthy of protection; we are made to be cherished, not abused. We serve those who harm us to our detriment, feeling that God always wants us to be martyrs for His sake. And yet in those abusive situations, we often find our identities as victims, something that keeps us stuck where we are, without growth and without a future. I know it seems strange that an abuser can be an idol. But the abuse often feels safe; it becomes our comfort zone. Venturing out, trusting God to provide, is far too scary. We'd rather serve our time.

Sometimes we control our family members because we idolize and idealize our perfect plan over the journey that God has laid out before them. We can't imagine being happy when others assert their independence. One mom I knew wrapped her teen as an idol around God. The two were almost equated. And when the teen left for college, this mother's world crumpled. No longer content with God and His new plan for her life, she gave in to depression and withdrew from everyone.

It's time we let go of people as idols. Not that we live fatalistically about others but that we realistically understand that God designed us to be filled up by Him first. If someone hurts us, we don't need to be freaked out or surprised. In fact, we should be surprised when people don't hurt us. This kind of letting go leads to freedom. If we are to be like Jesus, we need to watch what He did. He didn't trust humanity way down deep. He loved people, sacrificed for them, and empowered them, but He knew the gist of each person. We are a flawed species, prone to wander: "Because of the miraculous signs Jesus did in Jerusalem at the Passover celebration, many began to trust in him. But Jesus didn't trust them, because he knew human nature. No one needed to tell him what mankind is really like" (John 2:23–25).

The more we place expectations on people, the more they become idolatrous in our lives. We serve a jealous God, who will not allow us to worship people over Him. Sometimes He moves in our relationships in painful ways to remind us of this truth. I've shared this story in print before, but it's a great illustration of my point. When we moved from Seattle to East Texas, I was friendless for a time, which is a natural part of relocation. My friend Stacey back in Seattle became everything to me. In my desperate need for friends, I made her an idol. And when she forgot my birthday and didn't respond to e-mail in a timely manner, I shot off a diatribe to her. I even wrote about it in a veiled way in a support-raising letter. My intention was to show her just how awful she was at being my friend, even in a public way. Not my best moment.

She called me. And I'm so glad she did.

With sincerity, maturity, and firm love, she reminded me that she could not be my savior. "I make a terrible Jesus," she told me. As I realized she'd become an idol in my life, I apologized, and I asked God to please forgive me for running to Stacey first instead of Him. Today we have a mutually beneficial friendship, even miles apart. She is dear to me, one of my closest, sweetest friends. I love her all the more for telling me the truth.

We are not leeches meant to suck people dry for our happiness. We are people in need of a Savior. Even though we all try to be like Jesus, we can't truly be Jesus to others, nor can they be Him to us. Let's let Jesus be Jesus, place our expectations firmly on Him, and grant others the freedom to be human, to be blessedly themselves, to rid them of our expectations.

Place People in God's Hands, then Take Your Hands Off

In a similar slant, once we learn to worship God and not idolize each other, we run into a conundrum. What *do* we do? How do we love others? How do we interact, even after pain? How can we revere God in the way we embrace our relationships?

First, realize that not every friendship and relationship will last throughout your life. People change. Some move out of state. Others shift their priorities. Sometimes friends hurt you on purpose. And sometimes God moves you into new relationships for no apparent reason.

It's never easy letting go. But if we don't learn the art of relinquishment, we'll never move forward to embrace the new relationships God has for us. It boils down to trust. How much do you trust God with your relationships? Do you believe He is good? Do you have faith that He knows what is best, particularly when He moves you into a new circle of friends? Do you cling to some friendships longer than you should because of fear or insecurity?

To revere God—to hallow His name—is to trust Him at

this foundational level. God is a God of relationship. And He has a sovereign plan even in your friendships.

It's hard for me to get that sometimes. I have a subtle belief that every single friendship in my life must continue forever and ever, amen. I can't seem to let go, even when God moves me on. I view it as a failure.

I never liked rites of passage because they meant that once again, I'd be leaving friends. Graduations made me sad. Getting on planes to move away crushed me. And it hurt all the more because I seemed to be the one holding on long after a friend already let go.

I could berate myself over this tendency, or I could look at the deeper meaning. I love people. I need relationships. I adore community. And I firmly believe God created us to muddy ourselves in people's lives, loving them enough to tell the truth, sharing life together. This is all good. But sometimes life careens people in different directions, and as is the subject of this book, sometimes people hurt us in the process.

Instead of letting someone's rejection sideline us, why not look at it like this: God gave us that friendship or relationship for a specific time in our lives. We learned from that interaction. We had the privilege of loving someone else. That person enriched our lives for a time. But now it's time to trust God to move forward—still keeping an open heart in case God chooses to reunite.

That was what the apostle Paul did with regard to John Mark, the cousin of Barnabas. On his missionary journey alongside Barnabas, John Mark abandoned them early to return home to Jerusalem (Acts 12–13). His departure caused a rift between Barnabas, who wanted to give John Mark another chance, and Paul, who was through with him—which goes to show even Paul had relational stress (Acts 15).

Paul let go of John Mark and Barnabas, but eventually as God healed him and John Mark proved trustworthy, Paul reconciled with him and said to Timothy, "Do your best to come to me soon. For Demas, in love with this present world, has deserted me and gone to Thessalonica. Crescens has gone to Galatia, Titus to Dalmatia. Luke alone is with me. Get Mark and bring him with you, for he is very useful to me for ministry" (2 Tim. 4:9–11 ESV).

Like Paul, we'll experience heartache and disappointment with people. Sometimes we even separate. But God loves reconciliation stories. He loves to bring things back around to create wholeness and restoration. If you stay in a bitter state, you won't be open to seeing your relationships made whole.

I'm still waiting for some of my relationships to heal. Although I haven't been good and perfect and right in most of the situations, I have taken this verse to heart: "If possible, so far as it depends on you, be at peace with all men" (Rom. 12:18 NASB). All you can do is do your best to reconcile, to look at how you've hurt someone, to ask for forgiveness, then move on. You're not responsible for someone else's choosing whether to forgive you or to move toward you in relationship. Clean your slate first. Go to God, and ask Him what He wants you to do in terms of reconciliation. Then do it.

At that point, you honor God in the relationship. You take your hands off the relationship and place your friend (or enemy) into God's capable hands. You may never reconcile on this earth, but if the person whom you've struggled with is a believer, there is great hope in the life to come. There, the person will be all he or she should be, fully healed, fully free. And so will you. In the land of eternity and endless sunshine, that relationship will be fully restored.

REVERING GOD AND HALLOWING HIS NAME IN YOUR RELATIONSHIPS mean actively placing every person in your life in God's care. It means choosing to worship Him even when conflict sours a friendship. It means placing God above all other people and finding your ultimate fulfillment in Him alone. In that, you experience great freedom and joy.

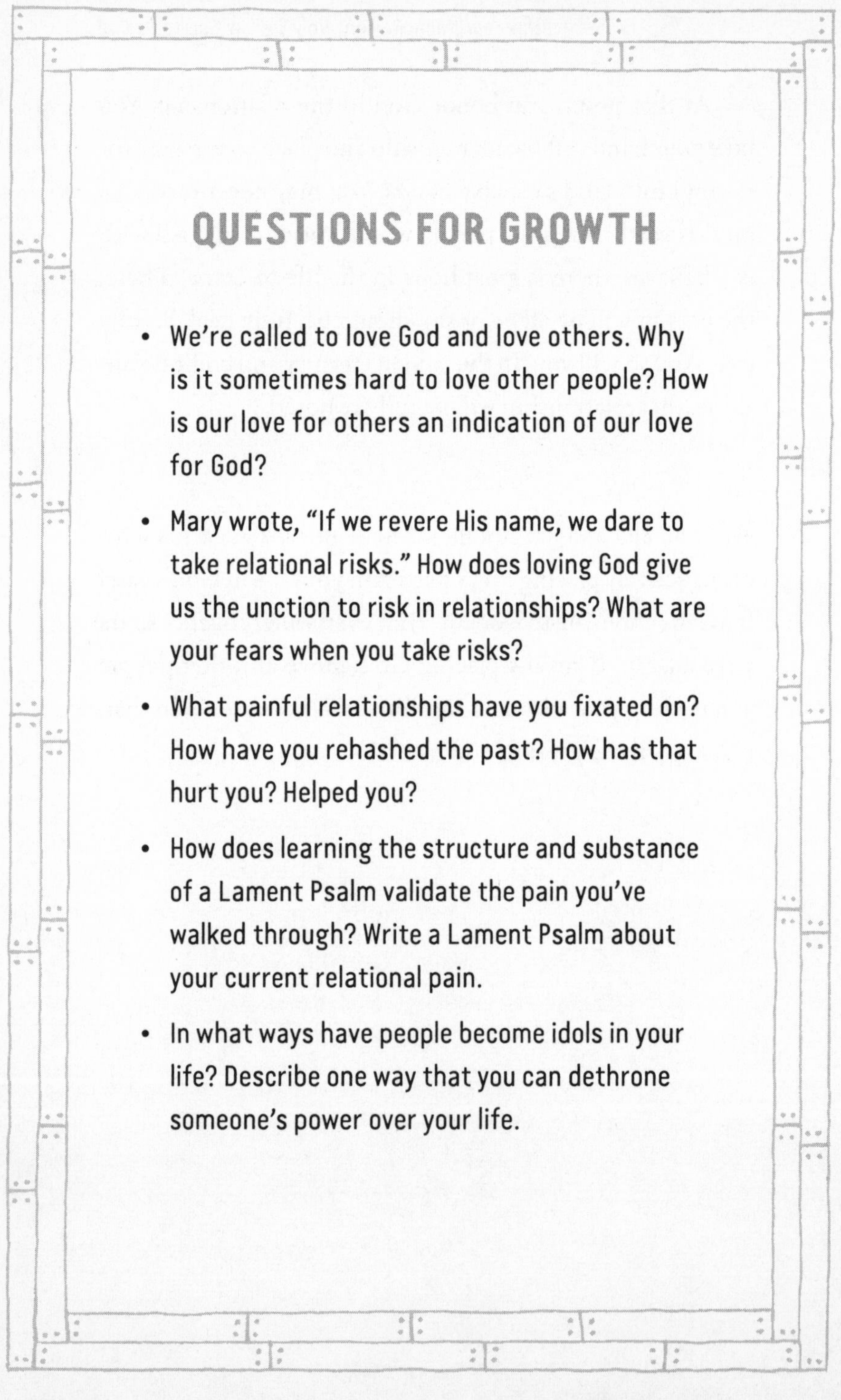

QUESTIONS FOR GROWTH

- We're called to love God and love others. Why is it sometimes hard to love other people? How is our love for others an indication of our love for God?
- Mary wrote, "If we revere His name, we dare to take relational risks." How does loving God give us the unction to risk in relationships? What are your fears when you take risks?
- What painful relationships have you fixated on? How have you rehashed the past? How has that hurt you? Helped you?
- How does learning the structure and substance of a Lament Psalm validate the pain you've walked through? Write a Lament Psalm about your current relational pain.
- In what ways have people become idols in your life? Describe one way that you can dethrone someone's power over your life.

"May Your Kingdom Come Soon"

Walk in the Great Right Now

THIS WEEK HAS BEEN TERRIBLE AND BEAUTIFUL, MIXED TOGETHER in one oxymoronic recipe. God has been leavening my heart in ways that frighten and excite. I've forgotten the irresistible nature of God's forward momentum kingdom, preferring to react to the past rather than be wooed toward the future. In my stress, I've let go of the nearness and immediacy of God's kingdom.

Let me back up a bit and share two brief stories.

My Home Growing Up

I GREW UP IN A HOME I DIDN'T WANT TO DUPLICATE. YOU'VE SEEN hints of that story here, but suffice to say, when I started having children, I worried. Incessantly. I fretted that I'd mess up my kids, that they wouldn't know they were cherished and loved. I relied on Jesus to help me change, and my prayer often was, "Help me not be like my parents." I lived in reaction to what happened back then.

Problem is, cautionary tales seldom grow you beyond a certain point. For a while I could exist off the fumes of my reaction to the past. I could use the deprivation in childhood to fuel my desire to be a different kind of parent. But eventually I stalled. Why? Because reacting to the past depended on my ability. What God wanted for me (for you!) was to give me something in the future to grow toward. It wasn't until I started dreaming of what I wanted my family to be and asking Jesus to give me His goals that I started growing again.

An Unhelpful Writer

IN MY TWENTIES, I HAD THE OPPORTUNITY TO MEET WITH A WRITER. I'd written hours and hours, miles and miles of unpublished words, but I didn't have a clue how to get those words in print. So I took a little notebook with me in which I'd penned several specific questions. I asked each one. The problem was, the writer didn't directly answer my questions, acting as if had she shared that information, something bad would happen, or I might be competition. I made a vow that day that if I ever figured out the secret of getting published, I'd share it with anyone who needed it.

So I lived that vow. I reacted to one person's stinginess by becoming generous with what I learned. In my thirties, when I finally figured out the publishing secret, I taught writers. I mentored many. I spoke at several national conferences, delivering a few keynotes. I set up two websites with the goal of helping writers. I created products to help writers create proposals. I even launched another mentoring website. But something shifted in me in the past six months. All the fuel—my reaction to the stingy writer—no longer helped me move forward. I received e-mails from writers wanting mentoring, and all I could do was pray for strength. My passion for this part of my career waned.

So I prayed. I wondered whether God would give me the beckoning goal that would enable me to grow through this lack of enthusiasm. Unlike what happened with my parenting journey, God didn't give me a new goal, a new direction. I had a choice to make. I could continue down this career path with little or no passion, or I could give it up.

As of yesterday, I gave it up.

How do these two stories connect, and how do they relate to the kingdom of God? This way: God wants to woo us forward to kingdom building. It's a greater motivator than anything else, including negative encounters. We can live in reaction to a negative relational experience and eventually stagnate, or we can ask God to compel us forward to a kingdom goal. Similarly we can become Christians because of our fear of hell, or we can follow Jesus in the adventure of living in light of the kingdom of God. See the difference?

Don't Live Back There

I'VE SPENT A GREAT DEAL OF MY LIFE LIVING IN REACTION TO THE past. And when I get stuck there, I grow bitter and tired. I burn out. I construct ironclad walls around my heart. But God wants more for our lives than merely surviving the attacks of others. He wants us to thrive in the aftermath, to become the kinds of people who help others thrive too. To move toward a proactive goal, not merely react to a negative circumstance.

Consider the disciples, how they moved from being influenced by the cautionary tale of Jesus' death to experiencing Jesus' resurrection and the sending of the Holy Spirit. Before the wow happened, they scattered, living in fear. They cowered and commiserated, but they didn't think of the kingdom. Instead, they concentrated on preserving their lives.

But then Jesus appeared to them, scarred hands, pierced side. He ate fish alongside. He restored Peter. Then He gave them instructions to wait for the Spirit before He ascended on a cloud to heaven. When the Holy Spirit fell upon and indwelt the disciples, something dynamic happened. The cowering and fear disappeared. Boldness and purpose replaced their mourning and woe-is-me words. And they turned the world upside down with the gospel, preaching the nearness of the kingdom of God.

The kingdom is the place where God reigns. When I look back on my parenting journey, I realize there were many times when I ran my own little parental kingdom, not asking Jesus to reign there but relying on my scrappiness to make things happen. I think back on my mentoring of writers when I assumed that someone being unhelpful to me meant I was supposed to become the queen of helping writers. Although I don't regret helping writers—it's a great thing to do—I do regret not jumping all in to what God truly called me to do—help people live uncaged, freedom-infused lives.

When we pray, "May your kingdom come soon," we submit ourselves to God's kingship over us. We let go of our assumptions about how we think our lives should go. We rely less on reacting to a negative past to fuel us and instead focus forward, compelled by the glorious future awaiting us. It's a positive, God-fueled way to live.

But what does that look like, particularly in light of the subject of this book? How can an irresistible goal woo us forward instead of living stalemated by the past? By looking at the kinds of kingdoms we're building right now.

The Woe-Is-Me Kingdom

MANY OF US LIVE IN THE WOE-IS-ME KINGDOM. IT'S A PLACE WHERE we rehearse the responses we never gave. Or rework the past with what-if questions. The problem is that all that ruminating doesn't bring life, and it eventually leads to over-introspection. By thinking only of our hurt in a relationship, we shut down our ability to be receptive to others' hurt.

I lived in this constant state of woe when we were in

full-time ministry. Several relationships chewed me up and spit me out and didn't seem to care that they did. In that space, I had no one to turn to except my husband, who was beset by similar discord. After battling a mysterious illness that went undiagnosed for months, having our house stolen from us back in the States by a con man, watching our kids struggling in school with angry, abusive teachers, I didn't need for my relationships to sour.

So I marinated in heartache.

And I stewed some more.

Until I felt completely overwhelmed.

I wrote long e-mails to friends back home. I Skyped with those who understood. But it wasn't the same as having right-next-to-you friends. In that despair, I walled myself off.

God saw fit to pull down the wall one day. We gathered at someone's house, and I found myself surrounded by the people who hurt me and kept hurting me. Part of me wanted to find a corner and read a magazine. Another part made myself get up and interact with the children there. At least that was safe. A young man came to visit that day. He'd been struggling with direction in his life, and I could see the effects of that struggle on his face and the way he held himself. I approached him, sat down nearby, and started asking questions. For an hour, I listened. In those moments a part of me enlivened. It felt good to venture beyond the woe-is-Mary world to see the angst in someone else. We ended our conversation with me asking, "Do you mind if I pray for you?" He welcomed it. As I prayed, I felt the energy of the Holy

Spirit and the love of Jesus for this young man. God poured Himself into me as I poured His heart into this person.

I walked away invigorated and changed. It's one of the best memories I have besides seeing our youngest daughter meet Jesus and be baptized in the Mediterranean Sea.

Michael Card nailed the beauty of letting go in his song "Things We Leave Behind" with this simple lyric: "We can't imagine the freedom we find from the things we leave behind."[1] What if the things we left behind are the bits and scraps of heartache others have inflicted? What would it look like if you truly let go of those words and actions that severed you? When you live in the woe-is-me kingdom, you see only those awful things. You cut yourself off from beauty and joy and hope. You sever your ability to empathize with others and build God's kingdom, person by person.

So take a risk today. Be willing to find someone to pray for. Take a moment to relinquish your pain to God. And place that person who seems to hold you back, who fosters introspective thoughts, in the hands of God. Ask God to move you from woe-is-me to blessed-is-me.

The I-Am-Awful Kingdom

THE KINGDOM STARTS FIRST IN YOU. GOD INAUGURATED HIS GLORIous kingdom in you the moment He chose you and you responded. Oh, how He loves you, cherishes you, leads you, honors you, and holds you.

Maybe you're not hung up so much on the abuse of

others toward you. Maybe you don't look back too much on that pain. Maybe you've picked up this book and felt, *Other people deal with this, but I don't. I forgive and move on.*

If so, that's good news. But there's more to it than reconciling with others. Some of us need to reconcile with ourselves. Our woe-is-me is actually instigated not by others hurting us but by us hurting us.

My hunch is that you're not interested in actively hurting others, right? I know I don't like to. But something happened last week that made me reconsider the way I treat myself. And I realized that the abuse I most often have to heal from is self-inflicted.

In the past few years, I've gained weight. Even though I'm in good shape, currently training for a half marathon, I still can't shed the extra pounds. I despise this. Holler at myself. Get frustrated. Curse my jigglyness. Eat less. Wince at the scale. But mostly I say mean things about my dilemma. Out loud. To my husband.

Poor man!

During one of my weight rants, he said this: "Mary, it hurts me when you talk that way."

His words stopped me. I thought about the times my friends have said similar things, ranting about something in themselves they didn't like. It pained me. Because I love each friend, it hurts to listen to each one abuse herself with condemning words.

Think of it this way: if you heard a mom hollering at a

child at the supermarket, and her speech was abusive, you would hurt inside. And you'd want to rescue that child. Now, make yourself the grown-up *and* the child *and* the crowd. Now you will understand why dissing yourself hurts you and others. And why it's so important to make peace with yourself so you can build God's kingdom.

If that's still hard to understand, imagine treating your best friend the same way you treat yourself (in your head). Think back on the abuse you've hurled your way just this last week. Below are some of the words I've thought about myself:

- *Why can't you budget your money more effectively?*
- *You'll never sell books.*
- *You should've approached your daughter about that hurt days ago. What kind of parent are you?*
- *Your garden has weeds because you're too lazy to weed it.*
- *You'll never overcome that sin.*
- *Other people will know about your inadequacy and share it with the world.*
- *Why can't you just endure? You're lazy.*
- *You're vain.*
- *Why can't you maintain your home perfectly?*
- *That dinner wasn't up to par.*
- *You'll never see breakthrough in your career.*
- *You probably deserved that abuse.*

This is just a smattering of the thoughts I've pummeled at myself. And as I read them now, I realize how caustic and damaging they are. I would never say those sentences to a friend because they're just so mean. When I build the I-am-awful kingdom, I tell God that He did a great job with every other human on earth, but He made a terrible mistake when He pointed to my mother's womb. Thinking this way insults the creative nature of God, and it demeans me to myself.

How do you get beyond self-abuse, moving from introspection toward living for the kingdom of God?

First, remember that God created you. Because of this, you have value. You are worth having others (including yourself) be kind to you. Because God shaped you, He dearly loves you. When you rant and complain about yourself, you lose and you hurt the God who fashioned you. Put simply, you grieve Him. When I see my daughter berate herself about a test at school, I hurt. In the same way, God hurts when you treat yourself poorly.

Second, realize that you hurt others when you hurt yourself. If you can't stop dissing yourself for your own sake, do it for the sake of those who love you. They don't like seeing you beat yourself up. It hurts them.

Third, realize that self-condemnation is not a fruitful action. Since when has condemning yourself made a positive change in your life? How has that truly expanded the kingdom of God? Remember the premise at the beginning of this chapter. We may be able to react to a negative for short-term gain, but it has no power to pull us forward. If you really want to grow, you must grow toward a positive goal. And that positive goal is finally realizing that you are incredibly free. In Galatians 5:1 (NIV) Paul reminded us that it was "for freedom that Christ set us free," and in the next sentence he shot a warning our way: "Stand firm, then, and do not let yourselves be burdened again by a yoke of slavery."

We enslave ourselves in the manner we talk to ourselves. But the truth is, God already set us free. He secured our release. To constantly hurt ourselves, resting in our inadequacy, is to call Him a liar.

In actuality, those words you utter over yourself are from the pit of hell. Jesus made this very clear: "The thief comes only to steal and kill and destroy. I came that they may have life and have it abundantly" (John 10:10 ESV). Look back over the words you hurled at yourself. Are they life? Do they help you move forward? Do they joyfully entice you to live an abundant life? Do they invite you to kingdom living? Or do they steal your joy? Kill your resolve? Destroy your esteem?

It's time to recognize, stark as it may seem, that when you abuse yourself, you participate in the kind of destruction that Satan wants for you. And he wins a victory because he keeps you so introspective that you can't see beyond the four walls of your prison of shame.

Stop abusing yourself. Not just because it's the right thing to do but because it's necessary for you to build God's kingdom.

Fourth, recognize that being kind to yourself helps you be kind to others and build the kingdom. Granting ourselves grace gives us gracious hearts toward others. We are to do unto others as we do unto ourselves. If we're critical of ourselves all the time, we naturally relate to others in that way. Ask yourself: Do I want to be a critical person? Really? And what benefit does a critical spirit have?

If you've been the one abusing, it's not easy to make peace with yourself. You can choose to stop hollering at yourself. You can learn to be kind to yourself just as you'd be kind to a close friend. You'll find freedom when you retrain your mind and mouth, and you'll discover you're becoming comfortable in your own skin.

The beauty about making peace with yourself is that it can actually happen because it depends only on you (unless you argue back). Jump outside yourself for a moment, and watch Mean You hurl words to Unsuspecting You. As the person above, watching all the verbal lashing, pull Mean You aside, look him or her in the eyes, and say, "I really need to move forward in my life, but your abuse is holding me back. Stop acting that way, or I'll stop paying attention to you. You'll be hollering at nothing. In the meanwhile, I choose to forgive you for all that abuse because I know how hard this life is. I hope we can be friends, but you'll have to learn to be kind first."

I know that sounds ridiculous. But so is chastising yourself to no end. Why? Because being mean merits absolutely nothing for you except lots of stress and inadequacy. It keeps you stuck. It hurts your relationships. And it stagnates your heart toward the kingdom.

The Narcissistic Kingdom

WHICH BRINGS US TO THE OPPOSITE EXTREME—THE IT'S-ALL-ABOUT-me kingdom, the awful realm of narcissism. I've had a fear about this kingdom hovering over me throughout my adult life. When I talked to my business coach once, I shared, "I'm just worried I'll get a big head and be one of 'those authors' if I step out."

She laughed on the other end of the line. "Mary, you know I'll tell you if you get that way. But I haven't seen that tendency in you, even in the past couple of years. You need to let go of that fear."

Where did that fear come from? Most likely from living in a family with narcissistic tendencies. It's crazy making, to be sure, to be blamed for everyone else's failures. I remember the one time a family member slapped me. After it happened, the person blamed me for getting slapped, though it was the person's rage that prompted the attack. I remember another time when I'd been called selfish for not wanting to do something that violated my conscience. I grew up believing that it was my responsibility to be perfect so that others couldn't blame me. It didn't work. No matter how much I tried, I never could be perfect. Any outburst or frustration within the household automatically became my fault. I so understood the pain of being blamed for someone else's anger that I didn't want to duplicate that in adulthood.

What is narcissism? Basically it means living your life with yourself as the sole filter, asking, what is best for me? People who struggle with narcissism actually aren't aware it's even an issue. They're happy with the world revolving around them, thank you very much. And they view everyone else as insubordinate. Consider these common traits of narcissism. As you read the list, keep in mind that this is the opposite of how Jesus interacted with people.

Narcissists . . .

- are passive;
- blame others for their faults or missteps;
- display contemptuous behavior toward those they deem inferior;
- envy anyone who has what they don't have;
- become overly reactive to personal criticism;
- lack a conscience;
- are highly critical of others;
- have a lifestyle of complaining and griping;
- are highly competitive and must win;
- are arrogant;
- coddle a feeling of grandiosity, living in a fantasy where they're a big deal;
- lack empathy completely;
- are authoritarian;
- are inflexible;

- feel entitled;
- are stingy;
- can be flirtatious and charming;
- consume themselves with appearance;
- are hyperconcerned about privacy; and
- exhibit a high degree of sarcasm.[2]

On the contrary, Jesus was active, engaged, interested. He gave joyfully of Himself, rejuvenating when He needed to do so in the presence of the Father. He did not use people for His benefit. He didn't need to. He was fully free to serve others, which is narcissism's opposite.

Any authority He had, He redirected to the Father. He chose to associate with people who would certainly not advance His standing in the community. In fact, He seemed to go out of His way to find the kinds of people whom narcissists ignored and offer them dignity and a voice.

There is no room in the kingdom for narcissism. But the acreage is wide and plenty for those of us who want to serve.

In terms of broken relationships and our hurt, narcissists will abruptly cut off those who hurt them or punish them through belittling. Neither of these strategies builds the kingdom of God. Cutting ourselves off from others protects us for a time, but often in the process we let that hurt fester into bitterness. (I'm not saying we shouldn't create sensible boundaries for those who abuse us, but that's an entirely different discussion. See chapter 8 for more information.)

Punishing others may give us satisfaction for a moment, but inevitably vengeance will corrupt us.

The Vengeance Kingdom

HAVING YOUR MIND OCCUPIED WITH THE KINGDOM OF GOD PUTS relational turmoil in proper perspective. But when you're consumed with what is fair and your sense of justice, you may slip into a vengeance-based kingdom. If a friend defrauds you, you defraud him. If someone gossips, you invent even better gossip to get back at her.

Vengeance is not the same as true justice, where we entrust our hurts to a faithful God. In true justice, we don't run around trying to manage our reputations in the aftermath of someone's untrue or hurtful words. Instead, we give everything over to the sovereign Lord, realizing that no one pulls the wool over the Almighty's eyes. God sees. He notes every misdeed. He watches the things we do to hurt others. He knows about those who steal and connive and swindle. And He's quite good at delivering justice.

When we dethrone ourselves from our kingdom and let God be God, great freedom becomes ours. We no longer have to make people pay for what they've done to us. We can rest—truly, fully rest—knowing that God has everything, every detail, within His sovereign grasp.

I've flirted far too much with vengeance, sad to say. In looking over my past and seeing one particular relationship,

I've had to choose not to entertain revenge thoughts. During these times, I remember Jesus' sobering words: "You have heard that our ancestors were told, 'You must not murder. If you commit murder, you are subject to judgment.' But I say, if you are even angry with someone, you are subject to judgment! If you call someone an idiot, you are in danger of being brought before the court. And if you curse someone, you are in danger of the fires of hell" (Matt. 5:21–22). Having angry thoughts is sin, plain as can be. Because murder first starts in the heart, actions follow. If we long for people to be hurt because of the way they hurt us, God deems us guilty.

When we stay in that place of vengeance, we disobey this amazing God who died for us, believing instead that our judgment is better than His. We usurp His rightful place as the Judge. Paul had strong words for people who live in the vengeance kingdom:

> Dear friends, never take revenge. Leave that to the righteous anger of God. For the Scriptures say,
>
> > "I will take revenge;
> > I will pay them back,"
> > says the Lord. (Rom. 12:19)

We must step away and leave room for God's judgment.

You can pray this simple prayer if you're stuck in the vengeance kingdom:

Dear Jesus, please forgive me for wanting to punish ________. I'm still very hurt by what ________ did to me, and it's hard for me to let go of that pain. But right now I choose to place all that pain into Your perfect hands. I choose to let You be the Judge, and I step back from my role as vengeance deliverer. Forgive me for trying to take Your place in this situation. I don't like ______, and I often have awful thoughts about him (her). But You died for ______. You love ________. My friend ________ is a human like me, making lots of mistakes and sinning aplenty. So I choose to grant ________ the grace You have so kindly given me. I choose to forgive. I choose to let You take charge of the situation. And I entrust everything to You in this moment. Amen.

The Survivor Kingdom

SOME OF US JUST SURVIVE. WE'RE NOT EEYORES. WE DON'T SCREAM at ourselves or bend toward narcissism. We have relinquished our desire for vengeance. So we may feel that we're okay in this kingdom pursuit. Except for this: we're numb, and we don't care that we are. In terms of trauma, there is an ebb and flow to recovery. After painful experiences, we shut down to better cope. We lose our personalities. We find ourselves preoccupied with nothing. Sometimes we sink into depression. We may self-medicate with alcohol or drugs (prescription or illegal). Or we turn to food or thrills or escapism—anything to withdraw from the world so we don't have to face our pain.

Although it does work for a while to heal and retreat from pain, eventually we have to choose to move forward. We can't stay in self-protection mode forever, nor will our lives be fruitful if we merely survive. There is more to life than putting one dogged foot in front of the other.

When we lived overseas, I spent two and a half years in survival mode. After nearly every relationship backfired on me, as friends became enemies, I shut down. Sometimes I couldn't make myself wake up. My bed became a haven from the peril of people. Thankfully my husband realized what was happening and started making me interact with people. I didn't want to. I wanted to make a blanket statement that every single human being on the earth, with the exception of my family, was not to be trusted and certainly didn't deserve my friendship. Had it been left up to me, this extrovert would've retreated into hermithood.

Jesus said He came to give us abundant life. This statement can be hard to swallow after people have wronged and abused us. When we're hurt, it's hard to see through the thicket of the pain toward the wide-open spaces of abundance. We smallify our worlds, choosing not to risk or venture for the sake of self-protection.

"I feel nothing," I told my husband during this season of self-isolation. "The anger toward the people who have hurt me has gone, but it's not replaced by joy. I'm living like a zombie, and all I feel is numbness."

Patrick listened. He watched how I'd shrunk within myself, morphing from vivacious adventurer to worried isolator. But his tough love eventually forced me to shift from survival mode to kingdom mode. It didn't happen overnight by any stretch, but I left the land of Numb and joined the real world again.

And now I find myself being surrounded by relationships, engaging with people, discipling others. I don't write this so you'll tell me how awesome I am. I struggled and gritted my way toward health. And Jesus pestered me like crazy, enticing me to trust others when my trust muscle had atrophied. He remade me in the aftermath. He moved me from lethargy to love. He wooed me from isolation to friendship. He encouraged me from safe living toward adventure.

God's heart for you is wholeness. He wants you to be more than merely a walled-off survivor. He longs to see you thrive in the aftermath of others' pain. And He understands. Jesus felt the sting of rejection from all of humanity. He experienced more abuse than we can comprehend. And at His most painful moment, the Father turned from Jesus for the first and only time in an agonizing aching of the godhead. Jesus understood betrayal like no one else, and He is waiting to move you beyond your self-protection into a life joyfully lived for others. This doesn't mean you'll never suffer. It certainly doesn't mean you'll never experience relational pain. But it does mean that you'll find yourself walking with Jesus, who walks behind you (where the abuse happened), beside you (as you process the pain), and before you in the glorious future (beyond the pain).

If you will allow Him, He will heal you, strengthen you, and give you the abundant life He promised. But first you must let go of the healing process, of managing it in your own strength. Give Him the reins of your healing. And trust Him to build His kingdom in you—a kingdom full of excitement, adventure, and risk.

God's Kingdom

GOD'S KINGDOM HELPS US LIVE IN THE RESULT OF OTHERS' ABUSE. IF we enamor ourselves with His purposes and His kingdom, we'll find ourselves better able to cope with pain. We'll no longer live attached to the past, as I did with parenting and writing. We'll realize that cautionary tales are poor motivators. In the Lord's Prayer, we're reminded to seek His kingdom, to be the kinds of people who long to see Jesus' rule on earth. With that as a thoughtful backdrop, read these words of another king, King David:

Hear my prayer, O Lord;
listen to my plea!
Answer me because you are faithful and righteous.
Don't put your servant on trial,
for no one is innocent before you.
My enemy has chased me.
He has knocked me to the ground

and forces me to live in darkness like those in the
grave.
I am losing all hope;
I am paralyzed with fear.
I remember the days of old.
I ponder all your great works
and think about what you have done.
I lift my hands to you in prayer.
I thirst for you as parched land thirsts for rain.

Come quickly, Lord, and answer me,
for my depression deepens.
Don't turn away from me,
or I will die.
Let me hear of your unfailing love each morning,
for I am trusting you.
Show me where to walk,
for I give myself to you.
Rescue me from my enemies, Lord;
I run to you to hide me.
Teach me to do your will,
for you are my God.
May your gracious Spirit lead me forward
on a firm footing.
For the glory of your name, O Lord, preserve my life.
Because of your faithfulness, bring me out of this
distress.

In your unfailing love, silence all my enemies
and destroy all my foes,
for I am your servant. (Ps. 143)

David's honesty here shows us that God gives us permission to feel pain fully without indulging it. He shares his depression. He complains. He worries. But by the end he says, "For the glory of your name, O Lord, preserve my life." He looks forward, asking God to lead. He appeals to God's glory and His great name. He asks for betterment not for his own sake but for the sake of God's fame. That shift from our kingdom to God's challenges us to live in the light of now, saving us from reacting to the past. We don't have to be yoked to the pain that others have caused us. We can be set free, through Jesus' wild love, toward a better, higher goal.

While the kingdom of God moves on in its crazy, surprising, amazing way.

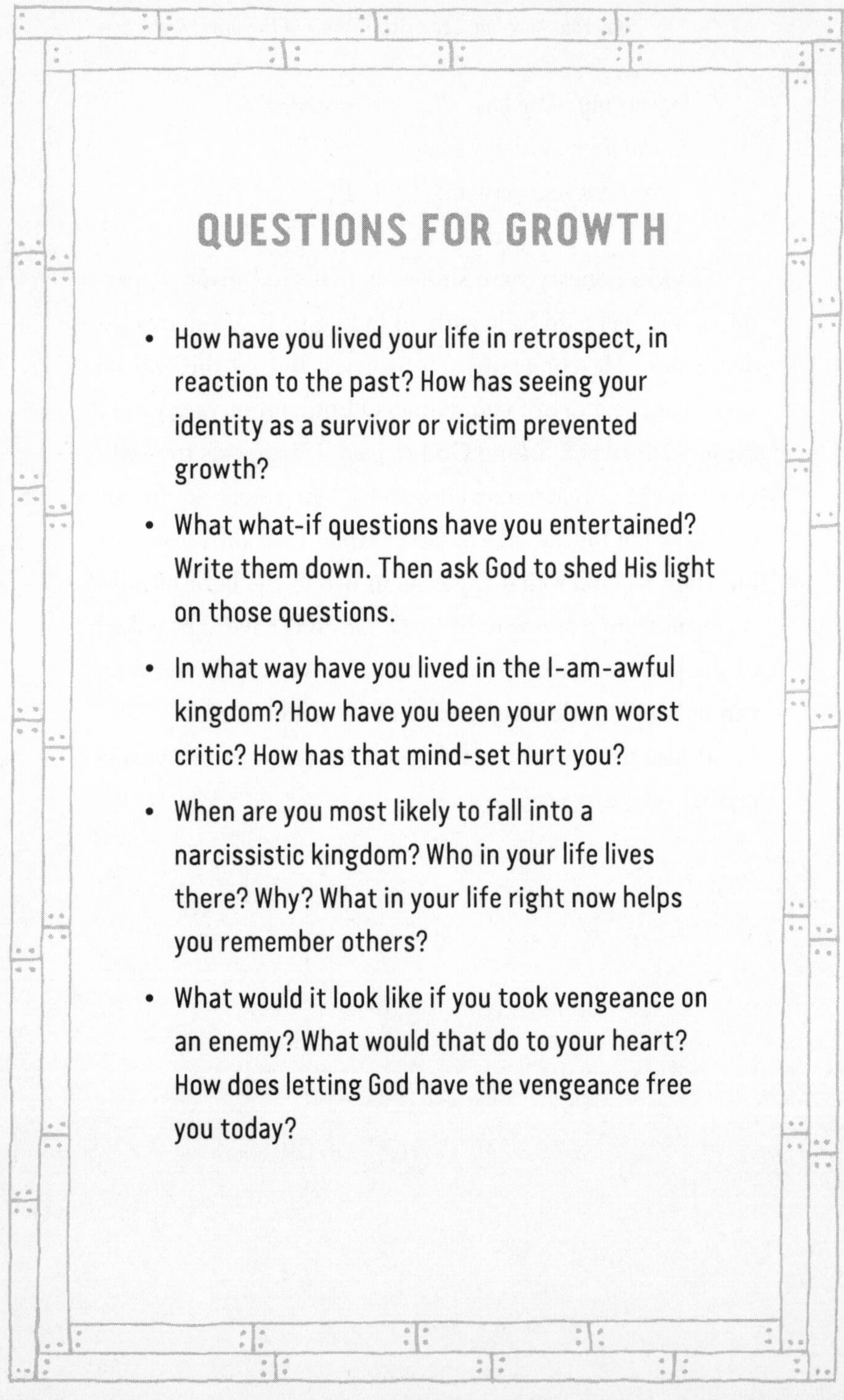

QUESTIONS FOR GROWTH

- How have you lived your life in retrospect, in reaction to the past? How has seeing your identity as a survivor or victim prevented growth?
- What what-if questions have you entertained? Write them down. Then ask God to shed His light on those questions.
- In what way have you lived in the I-am-awful kingdom? How have you been your own worst critic? How has that mind-set hurt you?
- When are you most likely to fall into a narcissistic kingdom? Who in your life lives there? Why? What in your life right now helps you remember others?
- What would it look like if you took vengeance on an enemy? What would that do to your heart? How does letting God have the vengeance free you today?

“May Your Will Be Done on Earth”

Respond Like Jesus

RIGHT NOW, I’M ON EARTH. HAPPILY SO. AND SOMETIMES I DON’T really want God’s will to happen in my life if I’m nakedly honest. I much prefer my way, my comfort, my lists accomplished. I like a manageable life, a tame God, and zero change because in that state I can do what I please, not having to rely on supernatural strength. Sometimes I deify my small strength and prefer it to God’s.

I want this in my relationships too. If I could order my life, I’d make sure that every friendship had joy, not stress. That every family relationship sang with hope. That my children would daily rise up and call me blessed. On this earth, I want harmony. And I want it *now*.

Yet Jesus asks for patience. Freedom in our relationships takes time, and sometimes conflicts don't resolve. While we can't guarantee harmony on this earth, we can run to Jesus to bring harmony to our hearts in the midst of our current tension. While we can't make people repent of their wrong, we can choose to repent of our own. While we can't demand that Jesus make everyone like us, we can ask Him to give us hearts that are kind to everyone we meet. The kingdom may not come (to our liking) to the hearts of others in the manner we choose, but we can always trust that Jesus can enliven the kingdom from within us, making us better parents, friends, children, and society members.

When Jesus prayed, "May your will be done on earth," we have to remember that He is the ultimate fulfillment of this prayer. The words He uttered heavenward were already obeyed words, already exemplified in His life. Jesus came to do His Father's will: "Jesus explained: 'My nourishment comes from doing the will of God, who sent me, and from finishing his work'" (John 4:34). It's an interesting thing for Jesus to say, especially in light of this prayer where He eventually asked God for daily bread. Perhaps our true sustenance comes not from chicken and vegetables but from fearless obedience and simple yeses.

Jesus learned this secret as He experienced hunger and want and disappointment and betrayal. He focused His heart and mind toward His Father, always seeking His will, always longing to please Him in all things. Even in His last days on the earth, Jesus reverted to this submissive prayer when He said this in the Garden of Gethsemane: "Father, if you are willing, please take this cup of suffering away from me. Yet I want your will to be done, not mine" (Luke 22:42).

Jesus reexplained His mission in the middle of His ministry, keeping things clear for us: "I have come down from heaven to do the will of God who sent me, not to do my own will" (John 6:38). In heaven, everything goes according to God's plan. Jesus submitted Himself to the Father, and the Holy Spirit interacted freely with both in a mysterious triune dance. When Jesus left heaven, He continued His track of obedience to show us what that would look like, to give us a winsome desire to do things utterly outside the box, to help us see that our religiosity gets us nowhere in terms of holiness.

As we contemplate this part of the prayer, we need to look to Jesus as we battle difficult relationships. We must ask ourselves, how did Jesus interact with people in every type of situation? Because He perfectly obeyed the Father, His actions serve as a map for those of us trying to navigate the infested waters of heartache.

How would He walk this earth? The answer? Simple: do what the Father does. Jesus explained why He acted the way He did: "Jesus gave them this answer: 'Very truly I tell you, the Son can do nothing by himself; he can do only what he sees his Father doing, because whatever the Father does the Son also does. For the Father loves the Son and shows him all he does. Yes, and he will show him even greater works than these, so that you will be amazed'" (John 5:19–20 NIV). Because the Father loved the Son, He showed Jesus everything necessary to live an amazing, holy, godly life. Jesus spent time with His Father, ascertained what the Father wanted Him to do, then did it. Which shows us just how important it is for us to maintain a minute-by-minute realization that the God of the universe resides within us and loves to direct us. He is the One who can make the kingdom of love come alive in our hearts. In this moment. For that person we struggle with.

We could spend hours examining every single personal interaction Jesus encountered, but since we're dealing with the aftermath of pain, let's choose a few instructive examples. Each starts with a common scenario (fictitious, but oh, so universal), then shows Jesus in the same situation. Watch how Jesus interacted with people, how He brought healing and hope, and how the kingdom of God advanced.

When People Question Your Abilities

JOSH BRISTLED WHEN BEN'S E-MAIL HIT HIS IN-BOX: "I KNOW you've been working on the data project all week, but I'm just not sure you'll finish it in time. I'm taking it over." Josh needed only one more day on the project, then he'd turn it in a day early. So he marched to Ben's office. Before Ben could say a word, Josh lambasted him, yelling what he thought of Ben's management style. From that point, they worked together with animosity and fear.

Jesus found Himself in a similar situation, only the stakes felt much, much higher to the disciples:

> Then he got into the boat and his disciples followed him. Suddenly a furious storm came up on the lake, so that the waves swept over the boat. But Jesus was sleeping. The disciples went and woke him, saying, "Lord, save us! We're going to drown!"
>
> He replied, "You of little faith, why are you so afraid?" Then he got up and rebuked the winds and the waves, and it was completely calm.
>
> The men were amazed and asked, "What kind of man is this? Even the winds and the waves obey him!" (Matt. 8:23–27 NIV)

When the disciples questioned Jesus' abilities, He didn't overreact or throw a tantrum. He displayed His power (which, of course, the disciples couldn't do) and chided them for their lack of faith. Jesus proved Himself to be the Lord of heaven and earth, controlling even the winds and seas, but He also tempered His display with words of instruction and truth. He dignified the disciples and kept the relationship intact.

When others question us, our first reaction is to get angry and defensive. Instead, we can do as Jesus did—stay rested. After we've calmed down, we can state our case in plain terms and without fanfare. It's okay to tell the truth. It's not bad to defend once in a while as long as we recognize that God is our true defender.

At other times when people questioned Jesus' abilities, He said nothing. His silence became the answer. This is what I love about Jesus. He didn't respond the same way in every situation. He was beautifully unpredictable. Why? Because every person He interacted with was a unique conundrum, and He knew best how to reach each one—by action, by silence, by admonition. It's important that we follow Jesus' lead—to be utterly receptive to the Holy Spirit so that our responses aren't robotic but Spirit enlivened, perfect for every situation.

When People Accuse

"YOU'RE TRYING TO UNDERMINE ME," CYNDI'S MOTHER-IN-LAW yelled.

"What do you mean?" Cyndi's heart pounded her sternum. She felt hot as the sun sank below the tree line. What had been a fun afternoon at the in-laws' home became a verbal boxing match.

"Every time I call your house, *you* answer the phone," she emphasized the word *you* as if it were a swear word.

"I'm usually the only one home. What else am I supposed to do?"

"Let my son answer it for once." Cyndi's mother-in-law moved in closer, her finger poised.

Cyndi backed away, tears wetting her face.

Since they'd come in two cars, she told her husband, Chet, that she wasn't feeling well and left.

Jesus faced many accusations. One such diatribe came after His disciples snacked on the original Wheat Thins:

> At that time Jesus went through the grainfields on the Sabbath. His disciples were hungry and began to pick some heads of grain and eat them. When the Pharisees saw this, they said to him, "Look! Your disciples are doing what is unlawful on the Sabbath."
>
> He answered, "Haven't you read what David did when he and his companions were hungry? He entered the house of God, and he and his companions ate the consecrated bread—which was not lawful for them to do, but only for the priests. Or haven't you read in the Law that the priests on Sabbath duty in the temple desecrate the Sabbath and yet are innocent? I tell you that something greater than the temple is here. If you had known what these words mean, 'I desire mercy, not sacrifice,' you would not have condemned the innocent. For the Son of Man is Lord of the Sabbath." (Matt. 12:1–8 NIV)

In this case, Jesus' response was firm and clear. He didn't run away from the accusation. Instead, He explained the Scriptures and pushed back on the Pharisees' wrong assumptions. He exposed their pride and hypocrisy. Many of us believe that to live as Jesus did on the earth, we must be silent, compliant people who always say yes to every request and give everything we have—even to those who bully and abuse. But here Jesus showed us another form of love—that of firm confrontation. You'll notice Jesus saved His choicest words for the religious elite, butting heads with those whom others perceived as holy. It's harder to go toe-to-toe with people like that. Bullies like to accuse, and they like to get a rise out of us. Jesus instructed us how to respond in an even, sweet-tempered tone, diffusing the accusation.

When People Reject

WHEN CHARLES BECAME A CHRISTIAN, HE FEARED TELLING HIS father. But eventually he couldn't keep living in deception about his newfound faith.

"I'm following Jesus now," he told his father.

His father didn't react. No emotion—whether rage or fear or worry—registered on his face. Instead, he stood up, shook his head, and left the house, slamming the back screen door.

Jesus faced something similar in His hometown where townspeople knew Him and expected Him to always be one way. They certainly didn't expect their neighbor to be the Savior of the world. So instead of welcoming Him, they rejected Him:

> Coming to his hometown, he began teaching the people in their synagogue, and they were amazed. "Where did this man get this wisdom and these miraculous powers?" they asked. "Isn't this the carpenter's son? Isn't his mother's name Mary, and aren't his brothers James, Joseph, Simon and Judas? Aren't all his sisters with us? Where then did this man get all these things?" And they took offense at him.

> But Jesus said to them, "A prophet is not without honor except in his own town and in his own home." And he did not do many miracles there because of their lack of faith. (Matt. 13:54–58 NIV)

Even Jesus felt the sting of rejection. It affected Him so much that His hometown's lack of faith stifled the work He would've done. We must realize that we're not alone when others reject us, particularly for our faith. Sometimes the people closest to us won't buy into our life change. The sad truth is that they will miss out on the "new us," just as Jesus' Nazarene friends missed out on His miracles. We can't make people welcome us. We can't force them to love us. We can't reverse rejection. But we can take heart that even Jesus walked this perilously painful path.

You'll notice through all these interactions that Jesus didn't shy away from saying the truth. And yet He loved those people. We wrongly think that telling the truth means we don't love someone. But grace and truth hold hands. Consider this verse: "For the law was given through Moses; grace and truth came through Jesus Christ" (John 1:17 NIV). Jesus had both: grace and truth, and both are elements of His love for others. If you love someone, you'll tell him or her the truth, not in a harsh or haughty way, but in a holy way—humbled and sweet. Jesus personified Paul's teaching about maturity: "We will speak the truth in love, growing in every way more and more like Christ, who is the head of his body, the church" (Eph. 4:15). If we want to be like Jesus, we'll let go of the fear of what others think and want the best for them. We'll speak the truth in love.

When People Are Full of Themselves

"I'M SO SORRY, BUT YOU CAN'T COME AND VISIT ME THIS WEEKEND," Brett told his mother. "I have a funeral to attend."

"What kind of son are you?" his mother fumed at him. "Don't you realize how much time I've spent planning this trip? You will not cancel on me!"

"Mom, listen. I need to be at this funeral. It's my best friend from high school. I thought you'd understand."

"I understand that you love your dead friend more than you love me."

Brett hung up on his mother, who was still yelling.

Jesus dealt with people like Brett's mother—people who can see the world only through me-first glasses. Watch how Jesus spoke about these narcissistic religious leaders:

> Then Jesus said to the crowds and to his disciples: "The teachers of the law and the Pharisees sit in Moses' seat. So you must be careful to do everything they tell you. But do not do what they do, for they do not practice what they preach. They tie up heavy, cumbersome loads and put them on other people's shoulders, but they themselves are not willing to lift a finger to move them. Everything they do is done for people to see: They make their phylacteries wide and the tassels on their garments

> long; they love the place of honor at banquets and the most important seats in the synagogues; they love to be greeted with respect in the marketplaces and to be called "Rabbi" by others. (Matt. 23:1–7 NIV)

We all know people who act like that (and to be honest, sometimes we act like that). Some gain their entire self-worth by being important, by lording their power or intellect over others. Again, you may be seeing a pattern in the way Jesus interacted with such folks. In this instance, He is distanced from them and sharing their modus operandi with His followers as a way of warning.

This weekend I received a call from an acquaintance. She wanted to know about a fellow business professional and whether I would recommend working with him. I knew the heartache he created over the years in business and in his relationships. Though I did not gossip (sharing details about why I know what I know), I did warn. Why? Because I felt burdened to protect my new friend. Jesus did the same thing here. He protected the disciples from people who loved applause, and in that He warned them not to become like that.

When People Wall Themselves Off

"WHEN YOU GO OUT WITH YOUR FRIENDS AND LEAVE ME WITH THE kids, I feel completely distant from you," John said to his wife, Alice.

"I need my space. Do you have any idea what it's like to

be with the kids all day and not get a break?" Alice paced the kitchen.

John poured some coffee for the two of them. "The past few months, I don't even know you. You're far away, and I can't seem to find you."

"I've been right here—doing your laundry, picking up after your kids."

He handed her some coffee, but she refused. He slowly emptied the cup into the sink. "I'm leaving." He grabbed his keys and stormed out the back door.

Enduring someone who has walled off his or her heart is one of the most painful situations in life, particularly when you're not sure why. John chose to walk away, to leave Alice where she seemed to want to be—in her secure compound.

But Jesus had a heart to pursue, even when His people shunned His tender touch. Listen to His lament:

> Jerusalem, Jerusalem, you who kill the prophets and stone those sent to you, how often I have longed to gather your children together, as a hen gathers her chicks under her wings, and you were not willing. Look, your house is left to you desolate. For I tell you, you will not see me again until you say, "Blessed is he who comes in the name of the Lord." (Matt. 23:37–39 NIV)

One key to keeping this kind of tender affection toward people who wall themselves off is proximity to the Father. He shoulders our bewilderment. He helps us love even when people walk away. He understands rejection. The other key is prayer. Jesus' lament here is a kind of prayer, a holy sadness sent heavenward. We may not understand why our friend has closed her heart, but God knows. And He can bring about heart change in His perfect timing. In the meantime, we need His strength so we don't give up.

When People Betray

"I CAN'T UNDERSTAND WHY I DIDN'T GET THAT POSITION," EMILY said. "I was qualified, and you recommended me for the position." She set down her coffee while a tear escaped her left eye. She wiped it.

Carla looked away. "I'm really sorry."

"But I don't get it. They didn't even offer the ministry to someone else."

"There is a reason," Carla said, "but I don't think you'll like it."

Emily felt Carla's words in her gut. She traced the corner of her napkin, then whispered, "Just tell me."

"Meredith shared in detail with the powers that be that you had an affair seven years ago. And they couldn't get past it."

Emily remembered sharing that awful part of her story—the sin that led to her meeting Jesus—with Meredith. She'd told her the story was a hard one to tell and asked her to please keep it to herself. And now. Now her sin had been broadcast to her church. What would she do when she saw Meredith again?

Jesus understands betrayal. One of His closest friends sold him out for a measly thirty pieces of silver. Pay close attention to Jesus' reaction:

> While he was still speaking, Judas, one of the Twelve, arrived. With him was a large crowd armed with swords and clubs, sent from the chief priests and the elders of the people. Now the betrayer had arranged a signal with them: "The one I kiss is the man; arrest him." Going at once to Jesus, Judas said, "Greetings, Rabbi!" and kissed him. Jesus replied, "Do what you came for, friend." (Matt. 26:47–50 NIV)

Did you catch that? He called Judas a friend. I can't imagine saying such a thing. Rat fink? Enemy? Evildoer? All those, yes, but friend? Even in betrayal, Jesus dignified people. I can almost hear the sadness in His voice when He said those words. He didn't resist; He resigned Himself, gave Judas one last kindness by calling him friend, then submitted Himself to the authorities.

That audacious grace floors me when I think of it. Allowing a kiss from an enemy, believing the best even when the worst is known. In this way, Jesus left the door open for repentance and renewed relationship. Have you ever wondered what would've happened had Judas come to himself in that moment, apologized, then tried to right the horrible wrong? Though Judas betrayed Him, Jesus kept an open posture toward His disciple.

When People Leave

"WHY DON'T YOU GO TO CHURCH ANYMORE?" ANDREW ADJUSTED HIS stride, then slowed to let George catch up.

"It's not worth it," George said.

"Well, I miss you. It's been a long time."

"Seven years." George huffed up the hill. "Since Mike died." George had lived angry ever since Mike died in a car accident seven years ago. He chose not to attend Mike's funeral, and he stopped going to church too. "The way I see it, God let Mike down. Let me down too. I don't need a God who takes people too soon."

Andrew stopped. Bent forward. Stretched his calves. "You think God should've prevented the accident?"

"Well, if He's so big and capable, He could have. So I'm either left with an incapable God or a God who is mean and arbitrary."

"Seems to me you're punishing yourself for how God acted."

"I really don't care," George said. He sprinted away.

When people leave us, grief assaults us. And that's okay. Sometimes people die. Sometimes circumstances remove them from us. Watch what Jesus did when a close friend died:

> When Jesus saw her weeping and saw the other people wailing with her, a deep anger welled up within him, and he was deeply troubled. "Where have you put him?" he asked them. They told him, "Lord, come and see." Then

Jesus wept. The people who were standing nearby said, "See how much he loved him!" (John 11:33–36)

Jesus did grieve. He wept about Lazarus's death. It's right to take time to grieve when loss comes. It's necessary and important. If the God of the universe wept, so must we. The problem comes when we shortchange our grief or, in the case of George, don't grieve at all. Bad things happen when we stuff our sorrow. Researchers say that the typical cycle of grief lasts two years: 730 days. 17,520 hours. 1,051,200 minutes. That's a long time to be sad. But it's normal.

In our culture of "always be happy," we forget the power and beauty of grief. Solomon wrote,

It is better to go to a house of mourning
than to go to a house of feasting,
for death is the destiny of everyone;
the living should take this to heart.
Frustration is better than laughter,
because a sad face is good for the heart.
The heart of the wise is in the house of mourning,
but the heart of fools is in the house of pleasure.
(Eccl. 7:2–4 NIV*)*

We grow because of grief. Although not fun, grief deepens our walk with Jesus; it makes us rethink the way we live our lives. It is a gift wrapped in a terrible package.

Joy will come. And if we are trained by grief, we'll emerge

on the other side wiser and steadier, unusually thankful for the process. Avoiding grief will only stymie our relationship with God and others. It will keep us tethered to the initial loss, embittering us.

So weep when someone leaves. Jesus understands. Let the process have its way. Cling to Jesus through it all, then walk out of it. Jesus didn't stay in the posture of weeping. He didn't let the untold grief He experienced walking this earth prevent Him from fulfilling His mission and calling. He kept walking. And so must you.

IN LOOKING AT THESE SCENARIOS, WE REALIZE TWO THINGS:

1. Jesus loves perfectly.
2. We are not Jesus.

The author of Hebrews summed up Jesus well when he wrote, "Think of all the hostility he endured from sinful people; then you won't become weary and give up" (Heb. 12:3). Jesus remains our ultimate example of how to live life on this earth, how to love the unlovely, how to forgive and move forward despite the pain inflicted by people. When we feel like giving up, we can ask for His help, trusting Him with our painful relationships. When we strive to be more like Jesus, imitating His counterintuitive ways, we begin to fulfill His will on this crazy earth. Being like Jesus is the pathway we walk toward becoming whole after people have hurt us.

QUESTIONS FOR GROWTH

- When was the last time someone questioned your abilities? How did that make you feel? How does knowing Jesus encountered the same thing help you cope?
- Why does accusation hurt? Have you accused someone else without cause? With cause? What happened? How might you invite Jesus into that conversation the next time?
- What happens to your heart when you experience rejection? What's your first reaction? What would you like your reaction to be?
- Jesus understood betrayal. How has betrayal affected you in the past six months? What has it taught you? What do you regret?
- Abandonment is one of the hardest things we face. When has someone leaving you put you in a tailspin? In the aftermath, what do you remind yourself of? How has Jesus helped you deal with people who leave?

"As It Is in Heaven"

Let Heaven Frame Your Relationships

WHEN JESUS SHARED THIS PRAYER, HE DID SO AS GOD INCARNATE, AS ONE who left the glory of heaven for the sweaty dirt of earth. He experienced God the Father's perfect will in a sinless place. And He breathed the peace of heaven, where relationships flourished in the light of God's love. "As it is in heaven" is a holy decree, a longing for things to be made right.

But as earthbound people, we tend to keep our thoughts grounded on earth, where our feet land every morning after waking. Thoughts of heaven interrupt only when we face tragedy, when a loved one nears heaven's gateway. In those times we realize there's eternality to this portion of the Lord's Prayer, a rhythm of heaven's breath as we consider our end and ponder what life must be like in the hereafter.

When I am dealing with someone who has hurt me, my first reaction isn't to ponder heaven or even entertain what God's will might be. My instinct is to wallow in the pain, not allowing heaven to frame my relationships. Instead, I get angry. I demean the person in my mind and calculate how much better I am than he or she is. (I never said my heart was pretty—more like petty.) Sometimes I gather others to hear my sob story so they'll also agree with my rightness. I build cases in my head, and I think ill thoughts about my friend.

All this useless activity precedes my finally running to Jesus, throwing the whole sorry mess at His feet, and asking Him to please-please-please help me think more heavenly about the situation. Paul encouraged the same thing: "While we look not at the things which are seen, but at the things which are not seen; for the things which are seen are temporal, but the things which are not seen are eternal" (2 Cor. 4:18 NASB). It's when I look at people through my eyes that I grow agitated and vengeful. But when I truly view them as God does, through the lens of heaven and eternity, I realize the small size of the offense between us. It's a blip. And my anger about the blip should shrink in light of that.

Thinking eternally helps us manage our pain, changes our expectations, and gives us purpose when we suffer. Here are five ways that cultivating a heaven-bent heart will help you endure relational pain and even thrive in the aftermath:

1. See the "Enemy" in Heaven

WHAT HELPS ME AS I GIVE MY PAIN TO JESUS AND ASK FOR A HEAVENWARD perspective is picturing the person who hurt me fully alive, joyful, and free, dancing on the golden pavement of heaven. Someday, Lord willing, my "foe" will no longer be ensnared by sin. He or she will be blessedly free of needing to hurt people for satisfaction. (The same is true for me. When I harass myself for acting poorly, I'm happier when I realize someday I'll be whole and won't be so prone to hurting others anymore. It's a two-way heavenly street.) When I imagine the person who hurt me as fully restored and worshiping the Father, I'm better able to love that person, to offer grace, knowing that his or her penchant toward hurting people will come to an end in light of eternity. This has been the single most helpful thing when I have trouble forgiving.

2. Remember God Woos Prodigals Heavenward

SOME OF US MOURN PRODIGALS. WE SPEND COUNTLESS HOURS fretting about a loved one who has snubbed a nose at the Almighty and seems hell-bent on personal destruction. In the aftermath, we crumble. When this happens, we need to reframe our thinking. Heaven isn't up to us. Heaven wasn't created by us. And we cannot woo our loved one toward a holy life. In light of that, our job is to surrender and place our prodigal in the capable hands of God, whose favorite job seems to be to entice prodigals to Him.

In the story of the prodigal son, we see the Father, waiting on tiptoes, craning His neck, waiting for the prodigal to return. But we also see His hand in the prodigal's circumstance. God constantly beckons us. Consider this beautiful verse: "All of us must die eventually. Our lives are like water spilled out on the ground, which cannot be gathered up again. But God does not just sweep life away; instead he devises ways to bring us back when we have separated from him" (2 Sam. 14:14).

It is God's job, not yours, to bring the prodigal home. And even God doesn't violate the free will of those who run far away from His grip. Realizing your helplessness, handing your friend or family member to the Hound of Heaven, will help you live with a modicum of freedom and peace.

3. Find Heaven Within You

WHEN WE LET THE PAST STRANGLE TODAY'S JOY, IT'S TIME TO STOP and find heaven right now. We live in the Great Right Now and the Not Yet. We groan for heaven and perfection, forgetting that the Holy Spirit gives us a dollop of heaven right now. We may not be able to control what others do or say, but we can control what we do and say in our relationship with Jesus. We always have the possibility of being close to Him. For those of us who enjoy control, this is good and bad news. Good in that we can opt to do something about our relationship with God, bad in that we can't change people.

It's our responsibility to court heaven. No one else can do that for us. I've learned (the hard way) that relational pain can either thrust me into the arms of Jesus or make me turn my back on Him. Either way, it's a choice. I can choose to cry on Jesus' shoulder, or I can give Him a cold shoulder. When a friend betrayed me, saying cutting words while looking me in the eyes—and wearing a knowing smile—I retreated to lick my wounds. I didn't retaliate in the moment, and for that I'm thankful. But I let her words poison my mind for several days. When my heart became embittered and threatened to harden, I gave the pain to Jesus. I asked Him to shoulder it, to sort it, to give me the strength to talk frankly and kindly to my betraying friend. In that moment, the burden of the pain lifted. But I had to make that choice.

The kingdom of God is within you. You have a choice to build it with an eye toward heaven and its permanent buildings, or you can tear it down, brick by relational brick. No matter what happens, you can grow your heart. You can ask Jesus to enlarge it for His sake. My friend Michele Perry reminds us, "No one can build my secret history with God for me. The level of intimacy I walk with Him in is a direct function of my hunger and desire. I can have as much of Him and His kingdom as I want. The question is: How much do I want? How hungry am I?"[1]

4. Let Heaven Frame Your Relationships

TODAY ONE OF MY WAYWARD FRIENDS CAME TO MIND. I FELT THAT familiar panic. What hadn't I done? What should I have done? Why weren't we close anymore?

The problem with that kind of thinking is twofold: I shift all the blame to myself and don't adequately assess both sides of the story. And I forget that sometimes God moves people out of our lives for reasons only He understands.

When relationships go sour (or we move away or someone changes), we don't need to become grabby and clingy. While it's good to at least have one conversation of exploration, it's not good to continually obsess over the change in relationship. Talk about it, then if you sense God giving you the go-ahead, move on.

God has new relationships for you. New friendships that will uniquely enhance and shape you in this period of your life. God has His reasons for moving you on (and moving your friend forward). Even if there's no closure, it's important to create closure in your mind. Otherwise, your head will constantly regurgitate what happened.

Ultimately, closure doesn't come in light of heaven. We may mourn a changed relationship here, but we can be assured that we'll have eternity to pick up the pieces and find joy in each other's presence forever. Thankfully, in heaven there will be no distance, moving, or relational discord. So don't fret. Don't wring your hands. Instead, relinquish. Here's a prayer you can pray when it's hard to let go:

> God, thank You for __________. You know I love that person. But I choose to release __________ into Your hands. Bring __________ back into my life at the time of Your choosing. Or not. But whatever happens, don't

let me get stuck back there. Today, please help me live in anticipation of the new friendships You have for me. And remind me that I will see ________ someday in heaven, where our friendship will be beautiful and free. Amen.

By God's grace, we can choose to let go of friendships that wane. Isn't holding on disobedience anyway? To cling to what God has moved or changed? God calls us onward, to cease looking back and revel in the relationships right smack-dab in front of us. Those people need our full hearts. They don't need our sadness over what once was. They need us present, loving, in the moment.

Thankfully, I'm learning to move into this heavenly, peaceful mind-set. And I've done it by praying. When Patrick and I met, we were friends with Matt and Susannah; in fact, we attended their wedding together while we were dating. Matt was my campus pastor in college and was instrumental in helping me heal from the past. His wife, Susannah, eventually became a terrific friend when I was a newlywed. She awed me. Such a woman of faith and beauty. And boy howdy, did she love to cook!

We moved away. Both couples had kids, raised them, went into ministry, walked through trials, and navigated life. So I'm not sure exactly when this started, but for years I've prayed for Susannah when I make dinner. I think about her love of cooking, and I pray blessings on her and her family. Praying for her makes me remember heaven. She's one of those friends I can't wait to hang out with for eternity. As one who can't seem to let go of friendships, even after moves, the thought of heaven brings a great comfort for me. I can imagine the two of us whipping up culinary treasures in heaven, laughing, catching up.

5. Live Today in Light of Jesus' Homily

WHAT IF JESUS CAME BACK TO EARTH TO PERFORM OUR FUNERALS? What would He say about our lives? We get a hint in Matthew 25:23 (NIV) when we read what the master said to his servant upon his return: "Well done, good and faithful servant!"

But what specifically would He say about your life? You'll start a growth revolution if you take a moment to think about the homily Jesus would give at your funeral. In this book we've talked about a wide variety of relationships, but let's consider some of our closest ones—marriage, parenting, and close friends.

What Would Jesus Say About My Marriage?

- Have I considered my spouse more important than myself?
- Have I learned the joy of backing down?
- Have I served?
- Have I shared my heart?
- Have I prayed with and for my spouse?
- Have I said hard things because I'm passionate about my spouse's growth?

- Have I assumed the best about my spouse even when circumstances dictate otherwise?
- Have I assumed my spouse understands what I'm thinking?
- Have I been fair in my fighting?
- Have I slipped into control and manipulation?
- Have I chosen to work on my issues?
- Have I talked about my spouse in a positive light in public?
- Have I demeaned my spouse?
- Have I resorted to cynicism or sarcasm?
- Have I set aside my agenda for my spouse's?
- Have I welcomed my spouse's dreams?

What Would Jesus Say About My Parenting?

- Have I taught my kids right and wrong by my behavior?
- Have I become the person I want my kids to become?
- Have I focused on launching my kids well?
- Have I demonstrated Jesus to my kids?
- Have I sacrificed?
- Have I seen them sacrifice for each other?
- Have I prayed for them?
- Have I engaged with them?
- Have I demonstrated the parenthood and love of God? Or have I created barriers to my kids' understanding of God?

- Have I shown grace?
- Have I taught my children to be respectful of others?
- Have I empathized with them even when it's hard to understand their world?
- Have I said hard things for the sake of their growth?
- Have I been consistent?

What Would Jesus Say About My Friendships?

- Have I loved my friends beyond platitudes?
- Am I interruptible?
- Am I confrontable?
- Do I foster fond affection and grace, or are my friends afraid to say hard things?
- Have I built in quality time with my friends?
- Do my friends know my affection for them?
- Have I dared to let them into the inner parts of my heart?
- Have I prayed with my friends and let them pray for me?
- Have I given good gifts?
- Have I let go of caustic friendships that influenced me toward evil?
- Have I listened to God about the state of my friendships?
- Would my friends call me forgiving and grace filled?
- Are my friends afraid of my negative opinions?

Asking these questions isn't a quick exercise. It's something you can do in a quiet moment of the day, perhaps on a personal retreat, where you honestly evaluate your relationships in light of eternity. These questions are not exhaustive. They're just a start. You may find more as you answer. Taking relational inventory in light of eternity won't be easy or pain free. Often it means seeing reality as it is. And truly if you want to grow, take this exercise one step further by asking your friends and family members to answer the questions for you. You may have a more accurate representation of where you are and where you'd like to be.

GOD'S WILL IS DONE PERFECTLY IN HEAVEN, BUT SOMETIMES IT'S hard to discern His will when we live in the land of heartache on earth. To pray that His desire would be accomplished here takes humility and a welcoming heart. I remember watching a show where a girl finds a wounded deer. The child asks a grown-up to fix it. He replies, "Fixin's hard." And it is. We're a mess down here, and fixin' doesn't always feel happy or easy. Fixin' takes time. Fixin' involves pain. Fixin' means we need to be brave. Fixin' might mean things don't turn out the way we want them to.

But when we get to that place, we can rest in the beautiful sovereignty of God. His will on earth as it is in heaven is an exercise in the faith of God's plan. He takes broken relationships and makes us whole in the aftermath. He uses the criticism of a friend to hone us. He creates discernment in us after we've endured deception. He fosters empathy in our hearts after others have damaged the tender parts of us.

Everything that hurts us on earth has the potential, when we let God put His hands in the conflict, to bless the world. In short, we hurt, and God heals, which makes us an agent of healing. In other words, when we're brave enough to let God transform our pain, we bring heaven to earth. Paul reminded us of this great truth: "Blessed be the God and Father of our Lord Jesus Christ, the Father of mercies and God of all comfort, who comforts us in all our affliction, so that we may be able to comfort those who are in any affliction, with the comfort with which we ourselves are comforted by God. For as we share abundantly in Christ's sufferings, so through Christ we share abundantly in comfort too" (2 Cor. 1:3–5 ESV). What I love about these verses is that He comforts us no matter what. That's the great denominator. And when He stretches His arm from heaven to earth, blessing us with comfort, we in turn touch our relationships with heaven's touch.

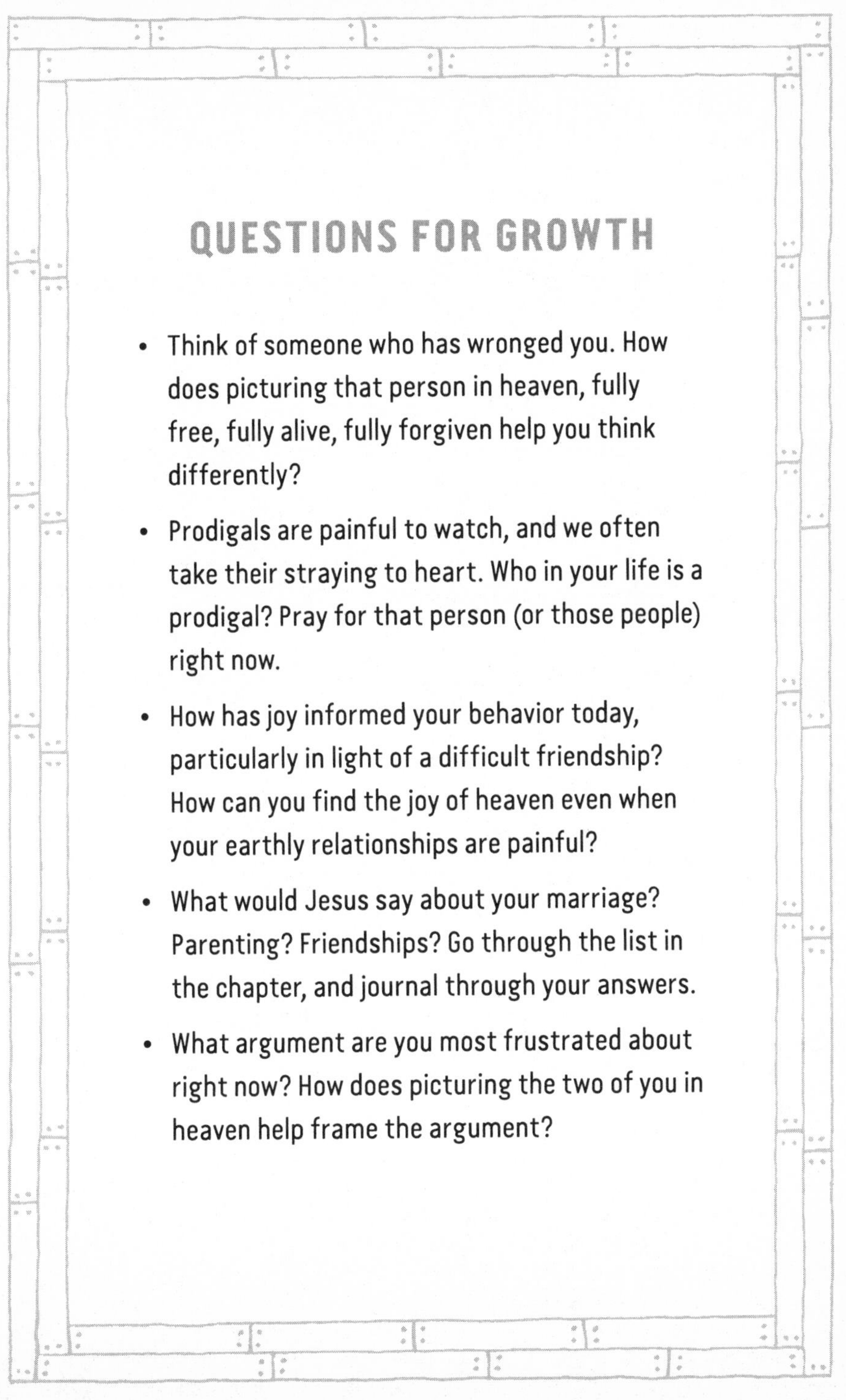

QUESTIONS FOR GROWTH

- Think of someone who has wronged you. How does picturing that person in heaven, fully free, fully alive, fully forgiven help you think differently?
- Prodigals are painful to watch, and we often take their straying to heart. Who in your life is a prodigal? Pray for that person (or those people) right now.
- How has joy informed your behavior today, particularly in light of a difficult friendship? How can you find the joy of heaven even when your earthly relationships are painful?
- What would Jesus say about your marriage? Parenting? Friendships? Go through the list in the chapter, and journal through your answers.
- What argument are you most frustrated about right now? How does picturing the two of you in heaven help frame the argument?

"Give Us Today the Food We Need"

Ask Jesus for Help

WHEN WE THINK OF OTHER TRANSLATIONS OF THIS FAMOUS PORTION of the Lord's Prayer, we often remember "daily bread" instead of "food we need." But according to most commentaries, those words don't merely mean ground grain, leavening, and water. Bread connotes everything we need to sustain our lives. It is the daily gift of God to give us nourishment for our bodies and our souls.

It's fascinating to note two words: *us* and *today.* We ask for this kind of grace for us, not just for me, which makes this prayer even more important for those of us who limp along after someone else's insult. All of us need that grace. All of us need forgiveness. Them and us.

And we need it today, daily. Yesterday is past, and the worries of the future are futile musings. Today is all we have, and God promises that He will meet us right now. Jesus said, "I am the bread of life; whoever comes to me shall not hunger, and whoever believes in me shall never thirst" (John 6:35 ESV). That's His promise to us, and it's in present tense.

It's important to understand Jesus' direct audience. The people were not wealthy by any stretch of our modern imagination. In that era, you were considered wealthy if you had one other set of clothes to change into and one meal lined up that you didn't have to work for first. They exemplified dependence on God for everything—even shelter for the night. With our glut of stuff, we can't imagine that kind of need for God. And yet He calls us to that moment-by-moment dependence.

Shane Claiborne wrote, "[The Lord's Prayer] is a prayer that the poor know well. It is also a warning to those of us who might pray for tomorrow's bread or those of us who might pray for a steak. We are not to pray for 'my' bread but to cry out with the poor for 'our' daily bread. We are not to pray for the poor, but to pray *with* them—and to realize that as long as anyone is hungry, all of us are hungry."[1]

Ultimately God calls us to live in the moment, ask for that bread, not let the pain of the past prevent us from engaging in the Great Right Now. How do we ask Him for such a grace gift for our relationships right now? And what does that look like as a lifestyle? Expanding the metaphor from bread to loving in the present tense helps us pursue "the food we need" in our difficult relationships. It gives us permission to thrive despite the desire to wall off our hearts. Asking Jesus for specific strength when we endure pain from others enables us to live openhearted lives.

Settle Your Worth

IF YOU DON'T LIKE CRITICISM, JOIN THE CLUB. IT'S NEVER EASY TO hear or read or experience.

And if I'm completely honest with you, I have to admit that I struggle deeply with it. I can't seem to move beyond it. Words stick to me like Krazy Glue, particularly negative ones. I assign weighty worth to them, more worth than the sweet words that God speaks over me. I grant negative words power in my life, over my thoughts. Rehashing all that criticism has to stop.

Because, thank God, our worth does not depend on whether we disappoint someone or fail to live up to others' expectations. We may feel that way, but that belief is untrue. Have you considered that it's plain old disobedience when you entertain mean words against you more than you accept and believe your worth? I'm not saying we should overlook criticism and fail to learn from it. As a writer I have to do that all the time. I couldn't improve unless I was willing to hear hard words. But we do have a choice when we hear criticism. We can listen, sift, ask God to help us, then change (or not change), or we can listen to the poisonous words and let them holler accusation over us:

"You're not worthy to be on this earth."

"You'll never measure up."

"You're not worth anything."

Those hateful words are not God's words to us. His words are *for* us. Yes, He disciplines, but always with hope and peace, not with berating, not by attacking our worth.

Criticism, whether it's accurate or not, does not define you. Jesus defines you. Even *you* don't define you.

Today choose to rest there. Not in the mean words. Not in your taunts. But in His delight over you.

Pass By on the Other Side

JESUS INSTRUCTED US THAT OUR BREAD IS FOR TODAY, NOT YESTERday. And really, all we have is this moment right now. Living in light of the past strangles our ability to embrace life freely today. That's why we need to let go of relational baggage. It should not define us, nor should the pain from it inform the way we interact with or withdraw from others today.

A few years ago, I learned a valuable lesson about today and the past as I jogged through my neighborhood, near the glint of sunshine on the lake, the smell of fall in the air. When I turned the corner to ascend the hill, I started the little game I'd been playing each time I did so. I condemned. Maligned. Hollered at myself.

Why? There's a house on my route that serves as a reminder of one of my failures. While I was at the pool with my daughter, I interacted with a parent. I'd completely forgotten that I'd met her before and asked her all sorts of questions I should've recalled the answers to. I noticed her perplexity. Only later did I realize I'd just treated someone I'd met before as a stranger. So every time I jog by the mom's house, words assault me: *You should've remembered her. Why didn't you?*

So I started my mantra to the cadence of my slow-paced run.

Then the Lord said this: "Pass by on the other side."

Really, Lord?

"Yes. You've beaten yourself up far too much. Pass by on the other side." So I did. I purposefully ignored the painful house reminder, steadying my gaze on the other side of the road. I noticed houses I'd never noticed before. New landscaping. A new vista. The sun shone differently on this side of the street. And once I passed the house, I felt free.

It really is true that you have a choice. You can run on the side of the road where the condemnation blossoms—where the yesterdays haunt you. Or you can choose to run to the other side and notice new signs of life today. You can beat yourself up or choose to offer grace. Yes, the grace to be kind to yourself.

Ask for Bravery

I'M NOT OFTEN BRAVE. BUT PART OF WHAT I NEED EACH DAY FROM Jesus is personal bravery. One day, I needed it for the sake of another.

The older gentleman standing before me in line at the

supermarket fumed. Livid about the price of strawberries and an apparent discrepancy in what the store advertised and what he was charged, he spewed venom on the girl who checked him out. Then he grabbed her elbow and told her to walk with him to the strawberry section to show her how wrong she was. Oddly, she willingly followed. While I waited.

The man returned with the shame-faced girl, waving the sign at her and hollering. I felt terrible for the girl, but I was also a little annoyed that all my groceries were on the conveyor belt and this conflict seemed to have no end.

Finally as a manager came near, I firmly told the customer, "Sir, I'm sorry you're having a conflict, but can you please take this to the manager here and have her settle it? There are people waiting in line."

He scowled. Later, my daughter Julia said she thought he would punch me: "Mom, if he punched you, I'd punch him back for you." But then she admitted, "That man scared me."

Back to the story. I looked at the checker in that moment, and our eyes locked. "Thank you," she said. "That man scared me. I can't thank you enough for rescuing me from him."

Her eyes, her fear, her sadness plunged me back to another memory when I was in the middle of a heated exchange where one woman berated and ridiculed a friend of ours. Something rose up within me in that moment. I said firmly, "You are not allowed to treat him that way."

Someone pulled me aside after that exchange and confronted me. "Mary," the man said, "you are reactionary. You need to control yourself."

At first I apologized. But after thinking about it and praying, I realized I had nothing to apologize for. Bullies should be challenged. If I hadn't, who would? Who would stand up for the victim? If Jesus were there, wouldn't He help the victimized?

I hope I did the right thing, both for the checker and for my friend. Sometimes it's hard to know. Because we're conditioned to think love is ooey gooey and touchy-feely. Always kind and gentle and sweet. I would argue that love looks pretty darn tough and even borders on mean in cases of protecting the innocent. Sometimes love looks an awful lot like using a firm voice and drawing a line in the sand and saying, "Sorry, but you're not allowed to talk that way to that person." It's the right thing to do. And Jesus will grant us that bravery if we ask Him.

Seek the Shelter of Jesus

HAVE YOU EVER COME TO THE PLACE WHERE YOU DON'T FEEL THAT you can take another sideways comment, ridicule, or criticism? I've been there. And I've had to learn to ask Jesus for help—otherwise I'd give up and become a hermit. When a disgruntled person sent my husband an e-mail missive, I chose to skim it and not let the words penetrate. And when I've received ill-meaning e-mails from angry people, I've tried to do the same. But sometimes those words penetrate, take up residence, and devastate.

That's when I turn to King David and his prayers. He wrote,

You hide them in the shelter of your presence,
safe from those who conspire against them.
You shelter them in your presence,
far from accusing tongues. (Ps. 31:20)

Being near accusing tongues is not my favorite way to spend an afternoon. I don't count them as daily blessings. But David assured us that God is big enough to shelter us from the accusing words that others send our way. His love and provision take the sting out of mean words. We can make it even easier on ourselves if we believe this. And we can grow through a painful interaction by choosing to let go of the painful words, whether by deleting (if they're written) or replacing our memory of someone's words with a prayer for him or her.

Rid Yourself of an All-or-Nothing Mind-set

I TEND TO DO ALL OR NOTHING. IF I TAKE A RUN IN THE MORNING, I make the whole day a healthy nutrition fest. But if I miss my run, chocolate lurks around every single corner of my house, making me eat it all day long. All or nothing.

Having this mind-set sabotages your relationships, though. Why? If you fail, you fail wholly. If you're an all-or-nothing person, one little mistake opens the door to widespread failure for the rest of the day. (Well, since I've eaten one chocolate-covered peanut butter ball, I might as well eat a dozen. Or, if I can't live up to my spouse's expectations, why even try?) Rooted in this is a strange form of perfectionism. If I can't be perfect, I might as well fail completely.

With an all-or-nothing mind-set, you tend to judge yourself relentlessly. A failure becomes catastrophic (even though it's not). The world crumbles around you, and Eeyore becomes your best friend. The problem is that relationships are seldom all or nothing. Often they involve the tension of good and bad, positive and negative. No one relationship is happy all the time. Nor is it accurate to say a relationship is 100 percent bad.

The other problem with an all-or-nothing mind-set is who you become when you're doing well. You can fall into the trap of pride and arrogance. When others don't live up to your expectations or standards, they become fodder for judgment. You may not say this out loud, but internally you'll wonder why other people can't hold it together as beautifully as you can. And you'll see those who struggle as less than. This is not the daily help that Jesus wants to give you. He gives spiritual gifts such as patience and kindness and long-suffering. He does not give a haughty, superior spirit.

Lapsing into the nothing category shortchanges your growth. When you give up and falsely believe that you'll never amount to anything, you stop risking, stop trying, stop growing. It causes atrophy in your spiritual life. And it devastates your relationships. Remember that God is the relentless pursuer. He pursues you. He pursues your enemies. In this very moment, He has not given up on you. So do not give in to despair.

Part of asking for what you need is finding balance within an all-or-nothing mind-set. By His grace, you give your all to relationships, holding nothing back, yet placing every heartache in the capable hands of your Savior.

Practice Contentment

DISCONTENT COMES MY WAY WHEN I LOOK AT OTHER FOLKS. CAN YOU relate to that?

I see someone else's house, life, ministry, books, successful relationships, and I begin to wonder why that blessing hasn't come my way. I hate to type this onto the pages of this book so you see the ugliness of my heart. I wish I could have a holy contentment for today, for what I have right now. Often I do, but sometimes my eyes stray, and I wallow in what I perceive as insufficiency.

The Lord often uses Scripture to bring me back into right alignment:

> Peter turned around and saw behind them the disciple Jesus loved—the one who had leaned over to Jesus during supper and asked, "Lord, who will betray you?" Peter asked Jesus, "What about him, Lord?" Jesus replied, "If I want him to remain alive until I return, what is that to you? As for you, follow me." So the rumor spread among the community of believers that this disciple wouldn't die. But that isn't what Jesus said at all. He only said, "If I want him to remain alive until I return, what is that to you?" (John 21:20–23)

Peter's eyes strayed toward another believer, John. He wanted to know what John's lot would be in the future. I can't help thinking an unholy curiosity resided there, a desire to see what God would give John, a place to compare. But Jesus didn't allow it. He plainly said, "What is that to you? You must follow me."

He says those words to me. To you. Right now. What does it matter if she has more than you? Why focus on his success? What's the big deal about how perfect her life seems? What is that to you?

We aren't called to follow after others' comings and goings. We're called to follow Jesus in the Great Right Now. Wherever He leads. Wherever He takes us. Whenever He calls. However He wants. In whatever manner He deems. We are called to look away from others and look toward Jesus. The nourishment He gives us is contentment in the moment that we are uniquely us, not them. That God sees us and will give us good and perfect gifts right now. He is a good Father who gives amazing gifts. But when we compare our lot to others, we forget the presents from God.

Choose to Engage Anyway

MAYBE WE STRUGGLE IN OUR DAILY KINGDOM PURSUIT BECAUSE WE don't fully chase after God's kingdom. Remember that we're called to balance. If you've been hurt by Christians and those injuries have sidelined you, examine your life and where you're spending your time. Is it all with believers? God calls us to support Christian community and to pursue those outside the kingdom. Perhaps you're hurting today because you've become too enmeshed in God's people, preaching to the choir, and not messying yourself with those who don't yet know Jesus.

Or maybe you're on the front lines of meeting non-Christian people, and it's burning you out. You find their behavior and attitudes encroaching on your walk with Jesus, and you're tired from fighting against it. Maybe you should retreat to your community of Christian friends, let them pray for you, and carry you through this time of fatigue.

We're not to retreat from the world.

We're not to retreat from biblical community.

God's kingdom is balanced. We are to be connected deeply with people inside and outside the church. Truth: both sets of people will hurt us. Both will manipulate, lash out, and confound. They are human, after all, just like us. The problem comes when we place huge expectations on Christians, then crash and burn when they fail. Although it is true that Christians should act better than the "world," it doesn't always work out that way. That old cliché "hurt people hurt people" represents both sides of the kingdom.

Living for Jesus on this side of heaven is hard. God calls us to engage with messy people within the church and hurting folks outside it. Yet God is big enough to shoulder either type of pain.

When we lived overseas, most of the relational pain we experienced came from other believers. We found surprising refreshment when we ventured beyond those walls and met with new friends and neighbors. Through our kids' school friends, we met a family who didn't know Jesus and had a thousand skeptic's questions. That family eventually moved toward faith in Jesus, and our daughter Sophie had the privilege of leading the daughter to Him. I don't know whether we would've pursued them had we not experienced such pain in other relationships.

The New Testament parallels this pattern. In the Upper Room, the Holy Spirit fell on the Jewish followers of Jesus. They became true believers in that moment, empowered by the Spirit to share Jesus with other Jews. Eventually (and quite quickly) the church grew in Jerusalem. But God used persecution and dreams and other means to push the believers beyond their comfort, to disperse them abroad. Then they interacted with Jews and Gentiles who had yet to hear about Jesus.

God won't let us stay safely in our churchy cocoons. He pushes us out. And sometimes He uses pain in the church to do that.

Understand the Season You're In

DISCERNING THE SEASON GOD HAS PLACED YOU IN IS IMPORTANT too. There are times to heal from relational discord, times to retreat, times to advance, times to invest, times to rest. For five years postministry, Patrick and I healed, two years for each one we'd served on the mission field. During that time of healing, our world became small. We trusted few.

We hoped to lead our children, discipling and training them. We committed ourselves to a small group of people from our church. Sometimes we went through the motions of life, still feeling numbed and devastated from the pain. We got angry. We took out our anger on each other far too often. We suffered in our marriage. We went to counseling. We tried to engage in deeper community but often pulled away, afraid.

We walked through a season of healing.

And just last week, God refocused us. We resolved to be relational again. We'd been protective far too long. And we'd navel-gazed, allowing some people within the body of Christ and their bad behavior to taint how we engaged today. You would not believe what has transpired since we decided to shift our focus outward again to people who don't yet believe and to the hurting.

In one week, I interacted one-on-one with ten people. People came out of every corner to find Patrick or me. We joked in our walk last night that once we made the determination to be about God's kingdom (instead of wallowing in self-protection), God brought many people our way, most of whom were hurting. We laughed about the irony as the sun went down and our dog panted in the humid June air. In a moment, someone drove a car nearly to the curb and stopped. It was our friend Kathy, who said, "Hey, I saw you, so I decided to stop and ask if you wanted to come over tonight and have some blackberry cobbler." We said yes, then laughed together at the uncanny season we found ourselves in. People were stopping along the side of the road to invite us to community.

OUR DAILY BREAD COMES IN THOUSANDS OF DIFFERENT BITES. I'VE highlighted only a few unique ways that God provides for us relationally. What I love about God is how He personalizes our lives. The daily Wonder Bread He gives you is different from the brioche He sends my way. The baguette He provides your friend tastes different from the Hawaiian toast He gives an acquaintance. Perhaps a lot of our discord and relational stress could be alleviated by recognizing the uniqueness of God in each other's life. Oh, the vast peculiarity of us all! And how tailor-made and clever God is to meet us in us-shaped ways.

Jesus' provision of daily sustenance reminds us of the manna in the wilderness. God "baked" it each morning, fresh and delicious. But if the people hoarded it, manna grew moldy and inedible. In our relationships, we can't go to Jesus once for help, then live the rest of our lives in our own strength; if we do that, our ability to love decays. We must ask Him every single day for help. By ourselves we cannot love, forgive, overlook, and grant grace. Jesus reminds us of this obvious but often overlooked truth: "I am the vine; you are the branches. If you remain in me and I in you, you will bear much fruit; apart from me you can do nothing" (John 15:5 NIV). With Jesus, we'll see fruit in our friendships. Without Him, our relationships will emaciate.

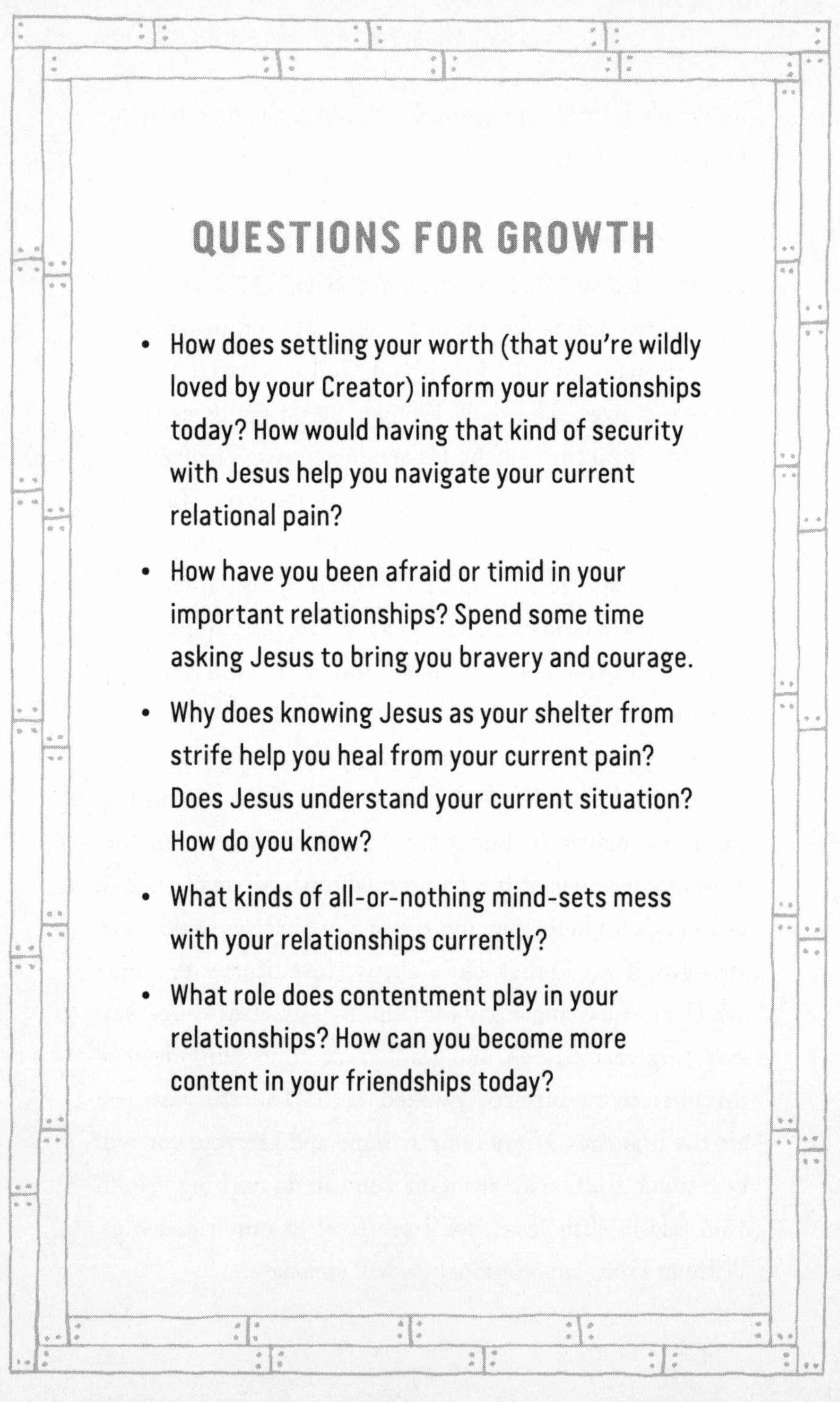

QUESTIONS FOR GROWTH

- How does settling your worth (that you're wildly loved by your Creator) inform your relationships today? How would having that kind of security with Jesus help you navigate your current relational pain?
- How have you been afraid or timid in your important relationships? Spend some time asking Jesus to bring you bravery and courage.
- Why does knowing Jesus as your shelter from strife help you heal from your current pain? Does Jesus understand your current situation? How do you know?
- What kinds of all-or-nothing mind-sets mess with your relationships currently?
- What role does contentment play in your relationships? How can you become more content in your friendships today?

"And Forgive Us Our Sins"

Be Repentant

WHEN WE'RE HURT, IT'S MUCH EASIER TO FOCUS ON SOMEONE ELSE'S heinous sins than to perceive our own sin patterns. It's natural to wallow in our pain and conveniently forget that we inflict pain on others too. In that place of victimization and self-righteousness, we fail to remember our mountain of sins against a holy and pure God.

But we must remember. Because a healthy awareness of our tragic shortcomings brings us to the only place we'll find help and life: the cross. In the shadow of the mighty cross, we all lie facefirst beside those who have hurt us, humbly able to receive grace enough to extend it to our friends and foes.

The hallmark of growing, vibrant, infectious Christians isn't their ability to abstain from sin. It's their willingness to let the cross highlight their sin so they can repent, ask forgiveness, and move on in light of Jesus' outrageous grace. Jesus doesn't require a sinless people. That's impossible. But He does ask us to be men and women after His heart, people who are honest enough to admit our failures, who actually need His strength to love others.

I met a woman who truly believed in perfection, and she mercilessly judged anyone who fell short of her perception of the ideal. Let's just say it's not easy to be friends with someone like that because you constantly feel judged, and you always worry you'll do something awful to offend. Throughout our friendship, I had a nagging feeling that something wasn't quite right. She said all the right Christian words. She held all the correct convictions. She pointed out others' flaws with precision. But she could not see her faults. Perhaps it was too frightening for her to admit them. Maybe if she slowed down enough to hear God's still, small voice, she'd realize how she fell short of His ideal.

No, she couldn't do that. Her security became her perfection, to the point that she honestly believed she was perfect. At that point, I couldn't speak into her life because how do you talk to a perfect person? How do you convince someone of sin? Inevitably that relationship crumbled. Even now as I type this, I pray for my friend who is enslaved to perfection. And I remember afresh how important it is for my sake and ours that I humble myself before God and ask His forgiveness.

I had a freedom moment in December 1987 (yes, in the bygone years) when I heard a ministry leader speak in

Urbana, Illinois. Like the friend I just mentioned, I falsely believed that for Jesus to really be happy with me, I had to do everything perfectly—particularly in how I related to others. He talked about his shortcomings in relationships in front of thousands of college students. He detailed his harsh words. He didn't do this to titillate; he confessed through tears. And he set me free.

In that moment, I realized that we all make mistakes. We all sin. In light of that, it's what we do with our sin that really matters. If we hide it behind a façade, we won't find freedom. If we pretend we're perfect, we'll live with deep shame. If we rationalize our sins or deflect them as the fault of the people who hurt us, we'll never grow, and we won't experience the freedom of forgiveness. Confessing our sins to Jesus and to others will set us free. Asking for pardon makes us dependent believers, and it shortchanges (thankfully) the part of us that thinks we're all that.

Pride has no place in the kingdom of God.

Oswald Chambers wrote one of my favorite quotations on this subject: "I am called to live in perfect relation to God so that my life produces a longing after God in other lives, not admiration for myself. Thoughts about myself hinder my usefulness to God. God is not after perfecting me to be a specimen in His show-room; He is getting me to the place where He can use me. Let Him do what He likes."[1] We're not statues in the perfection gallery. We're clay-footed folk who desperately need the God who made us from dust. Repentance and a posture of humility bring us to that dependence.

Think about the people who most remind you of Jesus. Are they perfect? Do they make you feel bad for not measuring up to their ideal? Or are they infectiously grace filled? Do they freely admit their mistakes? And when they confess their shortcomings, do you feel deep relief? In the presence of such people, the repentant ones, we find a safe place to be ourselves. We no longer feel alone in our struggle against sin. We can taste and feel and see and smell the grace that those people emit.

Since that's the case, let's become people like that. And let's examine the ways we sin when we're hurt and the ways we can foster a life of repentance.

Becoming the Holy Spirit

SARA CALLS HERSELF THE GIRL WHO DOESN'T CRY, BUT WHEN SHE recounted her story, she teared up. She told of a friend, Maggie, who knew her a long time. Maggie became suspicious of Sara's new friendships and concluded that she fell into a lifestyle of sin. Instead of coming directly to her, Maggie widened the circle, spreading untrue rumors—in the church. "It's hard for me to go to church," Sara said. "She didn't bother coming to me, asking me questions, or clarifying anything. Instead, she assumed she knew my heart."

In essence, Maggie took on the role of the Holy Spirit in an indirect way. She made a decision that Sara was living in sin because of the friends she kept. By assuming her friend lived a lifestyle of sin, she elevated herself and her perceived right understanding of the situation. Only God knows the heart. Remember what the Lord told Samuel when He chose a king? "Don't judge by his appearance or height, for I have rejected him. The LORD doesn't see things the way you see them. People judge by outward appearance, but the LORD looks at the heart" (1 Sam. 16:7).

We can't know hearts. Nor can we convict of sin. And when we take on that role as the sole purveyor of right and wrong, we sin. When we assume we know the contours of a friend's heart, we fall into all sorts of speculative traps. And when we let other people's perceived sin dominate our thoughts so that we either gossip about it or confront others in an unloving way, we open the door to heartache and misunderstanding.

In a rubber-meets-the-road example, I'll share my shortcomings in this painful area. For a few years during our marriage, I despaired. My husband spent time working through anger, and he didn't let me in on that journey. So I assumed all sorts of terrible things about him and his motives. At times I asked him what was going on in his head, but he didn't feel ready to share. In retrospect, I learned he's an internal processor, while I'm a verbal processor. I assumed his lack of response meant he was walking far from God. Then to make matters worse, I thought of ways to connive him back by going to his friends and asking them to please ask him what was wrong, by requesting that they pursue my husband. In short, I felt that his anger and the way he managed it were entirely up to me to fix. Not only did I try to be the Holy Spirit to him, but I invited others to do the same.

What eventually brought my husband back to a better understanding of his anger surprised me: he read a theological book. When he finished the book, my husband was a changed man. No manipulation, pleading, or requests for intervention convicted my husband. God had the path all along, but I tried to help God, offering Him a hand. Imagine that!

Assumption, manipulation, and conniving do not accomplish God's purposes in others. Want to know how to change others? Here's the secret: you can't.

You can pray. You can love. You can sacrifice. You can obey God. But other than that, you cannot convict someone of sin. And when you try, you assume God's position in your loved one's life. You shortchange the Almighty's plan.

Here's a prayer you can pray when you're tempted to play the Holy Spirit:

> Lord, I give You ________. Help me realize that You love ______ far more than I do. I'm frustrated with __________'s sin. I can't seem to get _______ to understand the depth of his (her) prodigal ways or how much his (her) sin is hurting me. So I take all that angst, and I give it to You. Take my pain in this situation. Heal my heart. Help me to be so attuned to Your voice that I'll immediately obey You. Forgive me for trying to be You to ___________. Jesus, please be You in _______'s life. You shaped ________, and You know best how to convict, lead, and love him (her). I give up my control, manipulation, and worry. I'm sorry for bringing others

into this. Help me to honor ________ with the words I say. And please help me see that my happiness isn't ultimately tied to _________'s behavior. Amen.

Putting Others on a Pedestal

WE SIN WHEN WE EXPECT OTHERS TO BE PERFECT, WHEN WE HAVE AN idealized version of people in our hearts and minds. Putting people on pedestals is a foundation for hurt and disenchantment, particularly when we elevate leaders. Typically this sin starts before the hurt, not in the aftermath. Still, it creeps in even when a friend disappoints us.

Our tendency as humans is to create archetypes. We want superheroes, people we can look up to and emulate. And secretly, we want to be superwoman or superman. Unfortunately aggrandizing others is building a house of cards that easily falls. Why? Because we're all terribly human and frail, and only one Person can live up to our expectations.

Life is messy. People are messy. That is why we need grace. But if we live in a perfect world, with expectations for perfect people, where will grace find a home?

There is a cult of Christian celebrity in the American church. It's ugly and pervasive. We flock to specific speakers, filling our tanks with their words, gorging on their pithy Twitter quotes. We chase after those whose ministries soar, who have large numbers of people in their e-mail distribution list or congregations. We demand more from them, begging for their time and attention.

Those celebrities run a huge risk of shipwrecking their faith in the process. Many have learned the secret that accolades mean nothing, but a few let the praise inflate their souls, making them inflexible and unteachable. I love what Michael Card wrote: "Never cease praying that you will not become a star or celebrity. Donald Davidson has said, 'Our culture places an absolute premium upon various kinds of stardom. This degrades and impoverishes ordinary life, ordinary work, ordinary experience.'"[2]

We do live an ordinary life, touched by the divine. The problem comes when we assign divinity to ourselves (and ask to be worshiped as celebrities in whatever circle we live) or deify others. In this sense, we are to live simple lives of love for others. H. R. Rookmaaker commented, "Christian freedom also is freedom from the sinful lust for money, from seeking man's praise, from the search for celebrity. It is freedom to help a neighbor out and give him something to delight in."[3]

Jesus came not to be served but to serve. And He asks us to do the same. We do not serve others well when we place them on a pedestal. In doing so, we practically invite heartache.

Avoiding Conflict

IN MOST MARRIAGES, THERE IS A FLEER AND A FIGHTER—ONE WHO flees conflict and one who seems to court it. Those of us who avoid tend to think our way is better. After all, if you avoid conflict, you don't have to deal with painful issues.

You can navigate around heartache and swearing and wrath. Doing this works for a time, but avoidance only delays the inevitable volcano of emotions and pain.

With our daughter's health issues of late, we had to face them head-on. If we ignored her headaches and pretended they didn't exist, they would still be raging. Only when we acknowledged them, took them seriously, and visited several doctors and hospitals did we begin to grasp what was wrong. Had we avoided her symptoms, she would've become sicker.

Many marriages and friendships suffer from the sin of avoidance. Those who struggle with this sin make harmony an idol. We had a friend whose spouse battled a difficult illness. Every time her spouse brought up the inevitability of death, she made a joke, laughed, or changed the subject. The reality of the pain was just too much for her. He eventually called us to intervene. "I can't deal with this anymore," he said. "I need to have a frank talk about my health."

Life is short. It's better to keep quick accounts with others because of it. We don't have the luxury of tomorrow. We can't know whether the next hour will come. Why live with unsaid words? Why prefer to live on the surface of life, never going deeper because we're fraidy cats when it comes to other people's emotions?

Others' reactions will not kill you. But unresolved conflict between you will fester and eventually destroy your relationship. It's time to be brave, to deal with the issues you face with kindness and grace and hope and a healthy fear of God. Entrust your relationships to Jesus; let Him take them. Give

Him your fear. And don't be afraid to share how you honestly feel, even if the other person has a habit of demeaning you.

Conflict stewed between my son Aidan and me. We danced around each other for weeks until he came into my office and told me how he was feeling. I'd been frustrated by his lack of initiative and his half-baked attempts at chores. He'd been angry with me for bringing up those issues in front of the other kids. We both had viable points. We both were upset and angry. The beauty of our conversation was that we left my office, both changed for the better. I understood Aidan's perspective, and he had empathy for my position. We prayed together at the end, cried, and saw God do very cool things in our midst. Aidan said, "Mom, I never knew that talking to you would help me sort out my problems." From that point onward, our relationship deepened and thrived. All because Aidan chose not to avoid conflict. All because we valued our relationship more than we feared conflict.

Reacting in Escalation

EVER NOTICE HOW QUICKLY A CONFLICT ESCALATES? IF ONE PERSON yells, the other reacts in kind. One person swears; the other swears back. In the span of about thirty seconds, a bantering argument morphs into a hellish war. You don't have to react in kind, though. You don't have to be held hostage by your tongue or your desire for retaliation. Remember, "A gentle answer deflects anger, but harsh words make tempers flare" (Prov. 15:1).

We can always choose to de-escalate. We can leave a room (not to avoid but to cool off so we can reenter the discussion at a better time). We can shoot a desperate prayer heavenward. We can minister in the opposite spirit. If one person accuses, we can do the opposite and praise. If someone takes our shirts, we offer our coats. Jesus excelled at this kind of creative disarming. He didn't play the games of those who wanted to pick a fight with Him. He pulled a coin from a fish's mouth to silence the tax critics. He brought a small child into the midst of the disciples shooing kids away. He drew in the sand while the adulterous woman awaited her demise.

As Jesus' representatives on this earth, why not be winsome? Disarming? Different? Unusual? Why not offer grace? When we're in the heat of an argument, we can choose to be the first to back down. We can reach a hand across the stony silence, welcoming friendship again. We can take the last seat and serve the person we're angry with. To do this is both counterintuitive and countercultural. We cannot have surprising and sweet responses if we rely on ourselves. Only a life fully attuned to the Holy Spirit can live this way. Which is a nice way to say, we have better responses when we're right with God. However, having grace in the way we respond isn't the same thing as enabling sin in a friend.

Enabling

SOME OF US READ THE SERMON ON THE MOUNT, CAMP ON TURNING the other cheek, and believe it's always right and Jesus-like to let people be awful. Unfortunately that's also called *enabling*. Enabling bad behavior doesn't show love. After all, do you love others well when you essentially nod your approval of their bad actions? If you love people, you'll want their highest, not be satisfied with their lowest.

Jesus told His followers to be careful about what is precious to them: "Do not give what is holy to dogs, and do not throw your pearls before swine, or they will trample them under their feet, and turn and tear you to pieces" (Matt. 7:6 NASB). There's a fine line between offering grace to people and letting them take full advantage of that grace. When we unknowingly entrusted the sale of our house to a con man and suffered foreclosure because of his actions, we didn't offer him grace. Why? First, because he didn't ask for it. Second, because he continued to violate us by trashing our home while we lived on foreign soil, unable to help our situation. And third, because he broke the law. Did we pray for him? Absolutely. Did we forgive him? Eventually. But did we ask him to handle our finances? Not on your life. We would've been giving our livelihood to a man who would take advantage of us.

That's an extreme example, but we sometimes offer too much grace in relationships. Someone violates us (or someone else), and we overlook the offense. We keep entrusting ourselves to his or her wily ways, hoping against hope that the person will turn around.

When I was a young mother who longed to be reconciled with my mom, I believed that I had to be perfect for her to meet Jesus. That perfection, in my mind, meant that I would be completely vulnerable before her. I'd forgotten this verse: "Watch over your heart with all diligence, for from it flow the springs of life" (Prov. 4:23 NASB). So I gave my untrustworthy mom my heart on a platter of my good intentions. Slowly I withered into myself, not knowing why I felt constantly condemned and unworthy. Whenever she hurt me, I took it. I internalized her words, letting them worm their way into my soul. I never, ever brought up her actions or words or opposed them in any way.

I didn't even realize I was doing this. Our lives enmeshed—she always right, me always to blame for anything wrong. By the way I lived and cowered, my mom became ten feet tall to me, and her opinions swayed my worth. During this time, I became very good at accepting all blame, feeling small, and longing for a shred of her approval.

I don't write this to malign her. She had no idea of the effect of our dynamic on me. I never let her know how her behavior hurt me, and I seemed happy to let her continue on in that path.

When my husband, my children, and I moved far away, the veil of what had been happening tore in two. I viewed objectively the dynamic between us. In light of all that, I also realized how emaciated my self-worth had become. When we flew home for our first visit as a family, I made a deliberate and frightening choice to be honest with her and set up a boundary. I did this with the full support of my husband

and through the help of a dear friend who saw my situation even more clearly than I did. What I feared: when I made my boundary and let her know how her actions hurt me, she would first retaliate and then withhold love.

I hoped that I'd been a drama queen, that all my fears were ultimately unfounded, and that she'd react in a positive way. But oddly it was right to trust my fears. I lived what Job said, "What I always feared has happened to me. What I dreaded has come true" (Job 3:25). She did get angry. She pushed back. She withheld love. She brought in others in ambush to tell me just how selfish I was for standing up for myself. You'd think that in the aftermath I would shrink farther within myself, but the opposite was true. Great, great freedom flooded into me. Though it certainly didn't feel like my boundary was a loving action, I had chosen to love my mom by telling her the truth, to no longer allow her to act in an unrighteous way. She didn't like my line in the sand, and I can understand her response. But she was no longer ten feet tall in my mind.

Enabling others in their bad behavior only lets them think acting wrong is okay. It's painful to step in and say, "Enough!" It doesn't feel godly or loving or fun. But it's the toughest kind of love I know. It's the kind of love where you truly have to abandon your agenda to God's, love His approval more than that of others, and venture forward into a relational minefield.

Is it worth it? Yes, yes, and yes. But giving up enabling is not easy.

Dehumanizing

WHEN WE'RE IN CONFLICT, WE SOMETIMES TEND TO DEHUMANIZE the person who attacks us, an increasingly easy thing to do in light of our Internet age. People become faceless in this paradigm. We take offense at things that were never meant to hurt us specifically, and then we lash out. I can't tell you how many insensitive comments, e-mails, and tweets I've received from people who suddenly forgot that I was a human on the other end, receiving the diatribe.

Part of this is a cultural problem, something I didn't discern until I moved overseas. There, I used to dread dinners with French people because dinner guests delved into politics, and a veritable opinion fest of banter ensued. Because I tend to view things in a win-lose way, I'd get stressed out when someone took a different opinion from mine. I wrongly thought the person talking hated me. Even more perplexing was that one particular friend affectionately kissed both of my cheeks upon leaving and greeted me joyfully the next day. I also noticed that the French didn't even mind what opinion they took. They'd switch to the opposite opinion just for the sake of great interaction and full exploration of an issue. They didn't dehumanize their opponents.

Our culture, however, demands a right person and a wrong person, a right opinion and a wrong opinion, a hero and a villain. If others dislike our opinion, they become enemies automatically, and we feel it's our duty to set them straight. Or we retreat to little caverns where other like-minded people hang out, and we spend a lot of time perfecting our correct opinions, reaffirming our rightness. Sometimes we even delight in viewing the other camp as evil, as unworthy of affection, as combatants. When we do this, we slip into dehumanization.

Dehumanization left unchecked can result in all sorts of atrocities. When we no longer regard people as human, we can demean, torture, end life, all in the name of doing right. This is the opposite of how Jesus treated people. His job as He walked this earth tended more toward taking dehumanized and marginalized people and giving them a voice, a face, dignity. We are less like Jesus when we categorize people into us-them groups, but we are more like Him when we invite those who differ into relationship.

In our current political climate, dehumanization takes a hateful turn. Jesus said we are to love our perceived enemies and pray for those who persecute us. He did not say we were to dismiss them, mock them, demean them. How we treat those who differ politically from us shows us a true measure of our maturity in Christ.

Paul made it clear that our battle on this earth isn't against people. It's against Satan and his demons. We run into problems when we forget that we have this very real enemy who is intent on our destruction, and instead we make humans that enemy.

My friend Ann is an author who writes beautifully, so much so that every paragraph seems to emit poetry. She has a heart bent toward Jesus, and her words invite us into the celebration that is Him. I love what she did in the aftermath of a critic's pointed review of her book. She invited him and his family to dinner. After she issued the invitation, the critic recanted his review, saying he'd forgotten that Ann was an actual person with feelings. He apologized for dehumanizing her.[4]

Ann's invitation to the table brings me back to those arguments at dinners in southern France. There, we realized there is no winner or loser, just conversation among friends. I don't need to demonize those who hold views different from mine. After all, I've held different views over time, and I bet if you look over your life, you'll shudder at some of your past viewpoints. We are a fluid people, changing our minds and opinions at will. But we all have dignity. We all deserve to be heard and loved and embraced. We all need to know we belong. And if we can't love those who differ from us, then what kind of Christianity do we follow? The winners-versus-losers Christianity? The I'm-always-right-and-you're-always-wrong Christianity? The Jesus-is-my-political-party Christianity?

When I'm tempted to dehumanize, I remember God's vastness and creativity. His mind is beyond comprehension. There is no possible way I'll ever think completely, 100 percent like God. And He creates all sorts of people to bear His image. In that holy collage, He reveals bits and pieces of Himself. No single person can hold the one "right" view. So we're all in the same boat. We all have touches and glimpses, and we're all on a journey together. Isn't it better to journey with others, listening to them without demeaning, fully realizing that we all need grace?

WHEN PEOPLE HURT US, WE FACE STRONG TEMPTATION TO SIN. AS you've read this chapter, you might have felt that I approached our temptations in a wishy-washy way. Don't confront, yet confront. Don't throw pearls, yet love those who differ. Avoid, yet say things. Set boundaries but don't exclude or dehumanize. I wish I could give you a ten-step list on how to navigate our relational stress, but I can't. The simple truth is that the best remedy I can find for not sinning in our painful relationships is to stay close to Jesus and be available to the stirrings of the Holy Spirit. When we walk in nearness to God like that, He not only gives us the power to do the difficult but right thing; He also gives us creative ideas on how to navigate pain.

Jesus loves every single person on this planet, including those who act like enemies in our lives. He knows best how to woo each person. So it's better to rely on Him when we're walking a painful road. Staying close to Him will help us love the unlovely, set appropriate boundaries with those who abuse, welcome political opponents and friends, and bless those who hurt us.

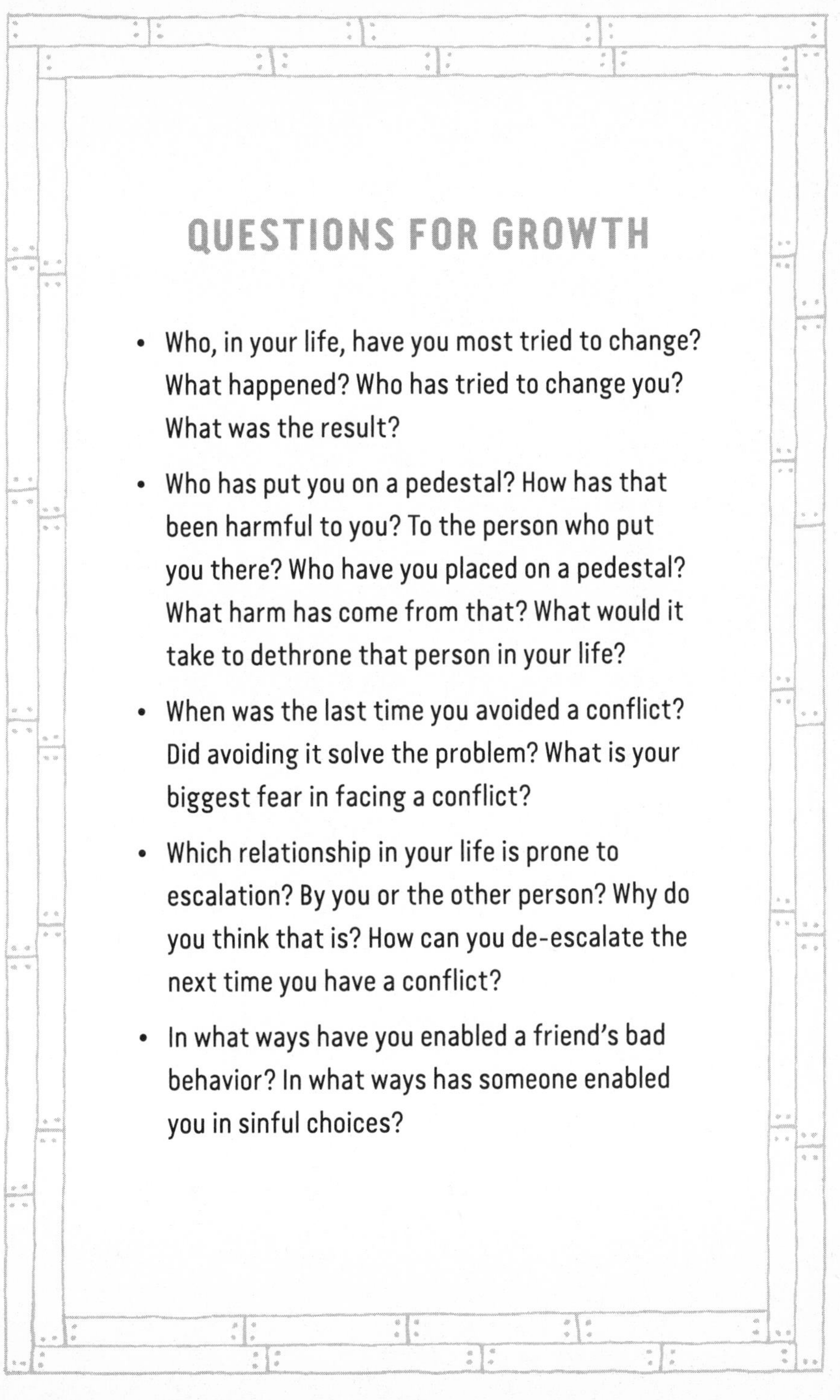

QUESTIONS FOR GROWTH

- Who, in your life, have you most tried to change? What happened? Who has tried to change you? What was the result?
- Who has put you on a pedestal? How has that been harmful to you? To the person who put you there? Who have you placed on a pedestal? What harm has come from that? What would it take to dethrone that person in your life?
- When was the last time you avoided a conflict? Did avoiding it solve the problem? What is your biggest fear in facing a conflict?
- Which relationship in your life is prone to escalation? By you or the other person? Why do you think that is? How can you de-escalate the next time you have a conflict?
- In what ways have you enabled a friend's bad behavior? In what ways has someone enabled you in sinful choices?

"As We Have Forgiven Those Who Sin Against Us"

Defy Bitterness

TRIALS ARE NORMATIVE IN THE LIVES OF BELIEVERS, AND THEY often come in the form of people. When people hurt us, we have a decision to make—to forgive or not to forgive.

We can get so caught up in others' sins that we forget to live our lives and move forward in holy momentum, particularly when those who hurt us are Christian leaders. I've spent way too much time wondering about how schemers and swindlers can remain in operation. Sometimes I sound like King David, writing psalms about all those who seem to get away with bad behavior.

But last week changed my perception.

I'd done the hard work of forgiveness. I learned to pray

for leaders who hurt so many and damaged the reputation of Christ. I prayed for the man who stole our house. But their lives and their seeming to "get away with it" still pressed in on me.

First, I remembered the man who swindled us. He died this year, though he was young and in relatively good health.

Then, I did a little searching on the others, and my findings surprised me. What I encountered when I cyber stalked them was this: a great diminishing. Not the sort of smallness you see with humility but a shrinking of influence, a decreasing life.

I believe that as we live for Jesus and continually submit ourselves to Him, we will enlarge. Not in a magnanimous way but in a John the Baptist way, where we understand we must decrease as He increases. And when He increases, our influence multiplies. Numbers 32:23 reminds us that God isn't blind in heaven, unaware of people's sin: "You may be sure that your sin will find you out." Although it often seems that people get away with their bad behavior, ultimately they don't. God sees. And eventually people who are caught up in repetitive sin, particularly the kind of sin that uses people and spits them out, run out of friends, and their circle of influence constricts.

Yet there is hope for them, for us. We don't have to settle for small lives. Author Stephen Mansfield believes there's a way toward freedom. He writes,

> I came to the conclusion that no matter how large or petty the cause, every religiously wounded soul I encountered

> was in danger of a tainted life of smallness and pain, of missed destinies, and the bitter downward spiral. And every soul I encountered had the power to be free, for each of them, no matter how legitimately, was clenching the very offense or rage or self-pity or vision of vengeance that was making life a microcosm of hell.[1]

Living in unforgiveness is hell. I've walked that well-intentioned path. After all, doesn't the person who hurt me deserve to pay for his or her sins against me? Shouldn't that person come to know the error of his or her ways and fall facefirst before me and apologize? When I walk that path, I assume the place of God, wanting others to come to me for what only God can grant. And in the process, I close my heart off bit by bit until it becomes a fortress that no one can scale.

Unforgiveness is the great isolator. When we obsess over others' sins, we swerve dangerously close to preferring our bitterness to the company of others. It shrinks our world until it consists of the offense and the offender—even if the offender has no idea we're angry. So really, our reticence to forgive leaves us alone with the sin. The longer we look at it, coddle it to ourselves, and ruminate on its effects in our lives, the more we become enslaved. And alone.

We are not built to carry offense. God designed us for joyful freedom. His intention is seen in the very first garden, Eden. Before the fall of man, Adam and Eve lived in relational harmony. No barriers existed between them. No arguments. No offenses. Just joy and peace and happy conversations.

This is God's highest will for us. But now we live in the tension of the fall, and we've grown suspicious. We've availed ourselves of feeling shame and hiding. And when another hurts us, our first thought usually isn't to seek harmony or offer grace but to get even.

Only a perfect person can carry offense and not let it affect Him. Which is why in our own strength, we cannot possibly forgive. We're not built for it. Our DNA courts revenge or withdrawal or punishment. But the DNA of Jesus trumps all our halfhearted efforts at dealing with sin. Why? Because He took on all the sin at once, once and for all. Because He could bear it, He did. And even as He bore our sin, He bore the sin of those who hurt us. This radical bearing of sin now enables us to ask Jesus for help and strength when we can't forgive.

And not only forgive but also learn to bless those who hurt us. Doing this is not intuitive. I love what Shane Claiborne wrote: "I find it very interesting that Jesus uses his harshest judgment on his inner crowd. After all, the only person Jesus calls 'Satan' is the soon-to-be rock of the church, Peter. . . . Jesus does exactly the opposite of what most of us do. Most of us find the best in ourselves and the worst in others. Jesus invites us to find the worst in ourselves and look for the best in others."[2] Only a radical forgiveness enables us to do that. When we come to the foot of the cross and truly realize how much Jesus has forgiven us (finding the worst in us), we can finally forgive others in light of that great gift—and begin to see the best in others.

I know it seems impossible, but it is perhaps the biggest measure of your maturity as a Christian. How well do you forgive? Do others see you as a grudge holder or a grace giver?

Paradoxically we cannot truly experience or know Jesus' forgiveness unless we choose to forgive others. Jesus told a pointed story about forgiveness. I've provided it from *The Message* so it is a fresh read. Read it two or three times to absorb its meaning:

> The kingdom of God is like a king who decided to square accounts with his servants. As he got under way, one servant was brought before him who had run up a debt of a hundred thousand dollars. He couldn't pay up, so the king ordered the man, along with his wife, children, and goods, to be auctioned off at the slave market.
>
> The poor wretch threw himself at the king's feet and begged, "Give me a chance and I'll pay it all back." Touched by his plea, the king let him off, erasing the debt.
>
> The servant was no sooner out of the room when he came upon one of his fellow servants who owed him ten dollars. He seized him by the throat and demanded, "Pay up. Now!"
>
> The poor wretch threw himself down and begged, "Give me a chance and I'll pay it all back." But he wouldn't do it. He had him arrested and put in jail until the debt was paid. When the other servants saw this going on, they were outraged and brought a detailed report to the king.

> The king summoned the man and said, "You evil servant! I forgave your entire debt when you begged me for mercy. Shouldn't you be compelled to be merciful to your fellow servant who asked for mercy?" The king was furious and put the screws to the man until he paid back his entire debt. And that's exactly what my Father in heaven is going to do to each one of you who doesn't forgive unconditionally anyone who asks for mercy. (Matt. 18:23–35 MSG)

The last line of this story should bother us, make us fear. We are called to forgive unconditionally those who ask for mercy. A high order, particularly when we're hurting. But a gateway for experiencing God's forgiveness. It doesn't seem fair, this duty of forgiveness. How can God ask us to do such a strange act? Why does He require us to lay down our need for revenge and embrace pardoning? Because He did the same.

Let's delve further into forgiveness. What does it look like? How can we do it? What if it seems impossible? Here are nine surprising things about forgiveness:

1. Forgiveness Makes You Act Counterculturally

I LOVE THAT FORGIVENESS HELPS US ACT COMPLETELY DIFFERENT from what people expect. Instead of rage, we offer a bouquet of grace. Instead of bitterness, we walk in freedom. Instead of treating people the way they deserve (in our minds), we treat them better than we treat ourselves. This is forgiveness' beauty.

David perfectly exemplified this aspect of forgiveness when he faced a very present enemy. Shimei, of the house of Saul, hollered curses and threw stones David's way because David represented the enemies of Saul. Watch how David exercised grace and forgiveness in the moment, and note how Shimei's unforgiveness rotted him:

> David said to Abishai and to all his servants, "My own son [Absalom] is trying to kill me. Doesn't this relative of Saul have even more reason to do so? Leave him alone and let him curse, for the LORD has told him to do it. And perhaps the LORD will see that I am being wronged and will bless me because of these curses today." So David and his men continued down the road, and Shimei kept pace with them on a nearby hillside, cursing as he went and throwing stones at David and tossing dust into the air. (2 Sam. 16:11–13)

David used his understanding of hurt to offer grace enough to ignore a man who dared to taunt the king. Even as the man hurled insults, David already knew pain. His own son wanted him dead. In that, he was the hurtee. He transformed that to empathy for the hurter (Shimei). We can do the same. When people try to hurt us, we can stop in the moment and remember that hurt people hurt people. We can take our pain and remember that the person hurting us is also in pain.

I also love that David entrusted himself to the Lord in this passage. He rested his future in God's hands and appealed to God's mercy. But he didn't demand it. He used the word *perhaps*. A lot of heartache in the Christian life could be alleviated if we used that word more often. *Perhaps* God will bless us today. *Perhaps* He will take note of our suffering and alleviate it. *Perhaps* my enemy will stop throwing dirt my way. *Perhaps* we will endure better today. David's response echoed Job's when he lost everything, which is interesting because in this scene David really lost everything, right down to his son's wanting his demise. Hard to imagine things getting any worse than that. But with Job, they were worse—he lost family, livelihood, home, and health. Then he said, "Naked I came from my mother's womb, and naked shall I return. The LORD gave, and the LORD has taken away; blessed be the name of the LORD" (Job 1:21 ESV). Job's *perhaps* rested on God's sovereignty and his steadfast belief in God's goodness.

All of life is a gift, whether we're happy about the circumstances or not. David and Job exemplify a loosely held life. It's not that God is capricious and uncaring; it's that He has a sovereign plan that only He truly understands. It's a good plan of mercy and joy and hope—one that ends in our ultimate sanctification. When we hold our lives loosely and give people the grace that God gives us, we can have the kind of confidence both men had.

They knew that God saw them, even when others didn't.

They knew God took note of the mess in their lives.

They knew God heard the words uttered against them.

They knew God had a bigger plan than their small role in it.

And so they were able to act counterculturally—to bless instead of curse, to rest instead of retaliate, to keep walking instead of fighting.

2. Forgiveness Comes When You Fast from the Turmoil

SOMETIMES WE CAN'T FORGIVE BECAUSE WE'RE IN THE MUCK OF THE pain, and we keep getting reinjured. If we stay in the midst of people's attacks, it becomes nearly impossible to pardon because the wound opens way up, always raw, always exposed. I experienced this with my family of origin. When I lived nearby and the injuries kept happening, I couldn't forgive. I didn't have the right perspective to even see the situation clearly. And every time I'd whisper a word of forgiveness under my breath, another frustrating and painful comment would take my breath away.

So we moved far, far away. And in that place of isolation and newness, I gained the perspective I needed to forgive. I'm not advocating a cross-continent move, but when it is possible, to remove yourself from a painful situation in order to heal and forgive.

Elizabeth went through this season as she moved on from a place of responsibility to a place of obscurity. In that obscurity, she found healing. Here's her story:

Hurt. Rejection. Betrayal. Disillusionment.

These were all feelings I dealt with after being dismissed from a job I had held for a long time. In hindsight, I see that it was time for me to go. I see that even in the hurt God was at work, moving me out of a place I'd stayed at too long so I could make my way into a new place, a better one. His place for me.

But those new, happy, free feelings were long in coming. And in the interim, there was a period of grieving the loss of my position, my identity, and coming to terms with the people who were involved. As I processed it all, I found myself drawn into conversations about what had happened, or what was going on in my absence. Talking about the organization I'd been a part of kept me feeling like I was still a part. By hearing the ongoing story, I got to keep being in the story.

I was putting off the inevitable severing that needed to happen.

Through several incidences and insights, it became clear that I needed to change some things if I was truly going to heal. I had to stop talking to the people in the organization—even though I liked them—and people related to the organization. I was no longer a part, and I needed to make a clean break. The only way I could see to do that was to go cold turkey. I texted, e-mailed or called the people who I'd talked with in the past, explained what I'd felt led to do, and asked them to please not send me Twitter status forwards, share stories of the latest developments, or in any way discuss the organization or its leadership. Initially I asked them for one week of radio silence. I was fasting from involvement in any way, shape or form.

That week became two, then three, and so forth. Eventually something did come up that directly involved me—a loose end that needed to be tied up. Because I had been through the fast and wasn't emotionally tied to any current issues, I was able to deal with that situation objectively and professionally. Emotions stayed in check and a resolution was reached. I know without a doubt that wouldn't have been the case had I not written myself out of the story voluntarily weeks before. I was proud of myself, and thankful that there had to be a way out of my misery, even if it took me awhile to see it.

Sometimes a clean break is hard to come by. Lingering feelings and unresolved issues can tie you up so much that you can't see a way out. For me that way out was a fast that ultimately led to freedom I could've never found otherwise.

3. Forgiveness Helps You Regain Positive Memories

WHEN I WALKED THROUGH THE LION'S SHARE OF HEALING IN MY twenties and early thirties, I couldn't recall a single positive memory of my upbringing. In retrospect, I found that fact alone a great indication that I hadn't yet experienced healing. But in my thirties, something wild happened. I remembered the piano my mom bought me one Christmas. I recalled the clothes she provided, patiently waiting for me to try on the next school outfit. Memories of vacations at the seaside, in the mountains, in a big city all came back to me. The negative memories had loomed so much that they'd dwarfed the sweeter memories.

In that space, I realized that we know we're healing by the number of positive memories that resurface.

I had the same perplexity with our time overseas. For many years, I couldn't recall a single positive memory. I couldn't even remember walking my kids to and from school—a big deal because they often came home for lunch, which meant four trips to the school during one day. I'd walked many miles on the cobbled streets of Le Rouret, holding my kids' hands, praying as they entered the wrought iron school gate. But for a long time, I couldn't bring those memories to the surface. What crowded them out were the faces of the people who had wronged us, the ones who had opposed us. My bitterness over those people and their antics sucked the air from any positive memories.

Recently I called the family together when I spied a house-hunting show where a couple and their four children looked for a home in Mougins, very near our little village. For the first time, I could watch the scenery of Provence.

I'm thankful that I could sit through the entire house-hunting episode and finally remember positive memories. The food. The sights. The beauty. The beach. The people. The language. The houses. Finally I smiled at the recollection—proof that God can heal us from tragedy and trauma. It may take a very long time, but it can happen. Learning to embrace a lifestyle of forgiveness helps usher in healing and positive memories.

Another way to reframe the people you're having a hard time forgiving is to invite Jesus into your most painful memories. While people prayed for me, I remembered a moment when I stood in a crib at four years old. I lived with my grandparents that year, and I have no recollection of my mother during that time. For my entire life, I believed the reason I was okay today stemmed from having a stable, loving home with my grandparents that year of my life. So when the memory flashed in my mind, I dismissed it as pedestrian.

But the moment I shared the memory, a flood of grief overwhelmed me. For the first time, I allowed myself to ask a few questions:

Why was I in a crib?

Why was I four years old, forced to take naps?

Where were my grandparents?

And why was I an inconvenience?

More memories came back to me—of going to bridge club with my grandmother and having to stay in a stranger's back bedroom, playing quietly so I wouldn't disturb anyone. Of hearing my grandmother's voice in the intercom telling me to go back to sleep. Of painful baths where my grandmother rubbed me raw. In that moment of recollection, I understood that I hadn't been truly wanted, that I'd been an inconvenience, a "have to." I wept while people prayed for me. And then Jesus showed up. In my mind's eye, I saw Him walk into the empty basement room, notice my uplifted arms, and lift me from my crib prison. He remade the memory for me. After all, it's true that God is everywhere. While it's never easy to reconcile God's omnipresence with evil things that happen to us, seeing Jesus in that memory redeemed it somehow. After that, I was better able to love my grandparents, be thankful that they took me in, and forgive them for thinking me an inconvenience.[3]

4. Forgiveness Fosters Empathy

SEEING JESUS IN THE MIDST OF THAT PAINFUL MEMORY ALSO HELPED me develop empathy toward my grandparents. I realized that I had been an interruption to their empty nest and that they, too, felt overwhelmed. No doubt having a four-year-old to manage must've tired them out.

When I first walked the forgiveness road regarding the boys who raped me as a kindergartner, I didn't want to forgive. What they did was horrific. Its ramifications resonate even now. Their heinous, dehumanizing acts have made me cautious, afraid, insecure, and torn. By God's grace, I've healed, but the scars remain. But I realized the more I hated them, the more I tied myself to those boys. Forgiveness didn't happen overnight (by a long stretch), but eventually it blossomed when I started feeling sorry for them. That empathy helped me forgive, and my act of forgiveness fostered more empathy.

Honestly if I met them today, I might yell. I'd probably

weep. But after that, I'd pray for them and tell them about Jesus. Because He's the One who bore all my sin on the cross.

If I don't believe that God's grace is big enough to cover their sin, I have a small view of God, of Jesus' outrageous act on the cross, and of grace. If I withhold forgiveness, I'll imprison myself. Grace extends to the victim and the perpetrator. It has to. It must. Because before a holy God, we all are perpetrators in need of pardon and mercy.

5. Forgiveness Doesn't Answer Every Question

UNFORTUNATELY EMPATHY DOESN'T ALWAYS COME OUR WAY AS VICtims of other people's sins. We share our stories and are met with blank stares or hurtful comments. Not everyone will understand your story. Not everyone will have empathy. And sharing doesn't always mean gaining a benefit. There were times I shared and felt violated in doing so. I'm not sure of the magic line needed before we're ready to share. For me, it was the difference between having to share with a gigantic need to be understood and sharing for the sake of setting others free. In between those two margins, healing had to happen.

Part of that healing came through wrestling with the *whys* of abuse, particularly in light of a sovereign God. If I believe God is omnipotent, loving, and omnipresent, I have a hard time reconciling why He would allow a child to be abused. After all, as a parent, I would do anything to prevent abuse in my kids. So why wouldn't God? I've come to the place where I have chosen to fast from the questions of *why*.

The truth is, He will redeem the pain. The truth is, He gives us free will, which means He also allows offenders free will.

What good can come from suffering? For that I return to Job, who lost everything—his children, his livelihood, his health, his will to live. He heard God at the beginning of his ordeal, but the Scripture says he saw God at the end: "I had only heard about you before, but now I have seen you with my own eyes" (Job 42:5).

That's what I want. To see God. And counterintuitively, I see God in the midst of my relational pain much more than I see Him in harmony. Those trials, which still don't make sense in my mind, drove me to God. Not finding appropriate love made me long for perfect love. Feeling alone helped me reach my hand to a God who was there. When I think about it that way, I begin to thank God for the trials because they plunge me back into His embrace.

But the questions remain. Particularly the *whys*. Even when I forgive, they niggle at the back of my mind. Sometimes I return to those sad places, those questioning places. I truly don't know why awful things happen to us. On this earth we will live in the tension of that gnawing question.

6. Forgiveness Isn't Cheap Grace

WHICH IS WHY WE NEED TO DISCERN THE DIFFERENCE BETWEEN cheap and real grace. I can't describe how angry I get when I hear about people being ignored or shunned or silenced.

Something akin to a holy roar rises up inside me. Once, a well-meaning friend excused a man who may have been hurting children (we couldn't prove it). "You need to offer more grace," he said.

I did not agree. Since when is it okay to give grace to someone who has a choice to offend or not, particularly when that adult hurts a child? Shouldn't grace be extended more freely to the vulnerable who had no choice in the matter? I'm not talking about an adult who realizes what he or she has done is wrong and seeks to ask forgiveness. I'm referring to a culture of community where we give preference to the one who is sinning because to get involved is just too hard, too sticky, too risky, too much work, too much stress. Giving grace to the unrepentant offender is offering cheap grace.

Dietrich Bonhoeffer, the German theologian who died for his faith in World War II, wrote, "Cheap grace is the preaching of forgiveness without requiring repentance, baptism without church discipline, communion without confession, absolution without personal confession. Cheap grace is grace without discipleship, grace without the cross, grace without Jesus Christ."[4]

Real grace forces sin out to the forefront, calls it the hellish thing it is, and applies redemption in healthy doses. It's calling abuse what it is: enslaving, violating, dehumanizing. It's bringing it to the light of day, no longer shoving it in the back room of hushed conversations. Grace happens in that vulnerable, real space.

Some will say that people who offend can't help it. But I

know from personal experience that's not a viable excuse. I was violated as a child, yet I don't violate. There are millions of victims out there who grow up, heal, and do not perpetrate. And as long as we turn our eyes away from those who inflict harm on the vulnerable, we, in a sense, validate the abuse as normative.

It's not okay.

It's sin.

And it *must* stop.

The conundrum comes when we equate forgiveness with judicial pardon. While it's good and right for us to forgive those who hurt us, it's also good and right when a perpetrator of a crime finds justice. We forgive so we won't be imprisoned by bitterness, but that doesn't mean we eliminate the possibility of prison for people who break the law. Forgiveness is for our sake. Justice is for society's sake.

7. Forgiveness Reminds You of Your Need

SINCE FORGIVENESS IS FOR OUR SAKE, GOD REMINDS US OF OUR NEED for it when we offer it. It's easy for me to slip into victimhood, seeing everyone as mean and bad and me as the heroine of my epic story. But the truth is, I'm a villain too.

J. B. Phillips translates one of my favorite passages this way: "We have no superhuman High Priest to whom our weaknesses are unintelligible—he himself has shared fully in all our experience of temptation, except that he never sinned. Let us therefore approach the throne of grace with fullest confidence, that we may receive mercy for our failures and grace to help in the hour of need" (Heb. 4:15–16 PHILLIPS).

When I sin, He is there because He was tempted by the tempter extraordinaire and came out unscathed. When others sin against me, He is there because He felt the inhuman weight of humanity's depravity on His holy shoulders. When I'm alone, He is there because He stood alone on this earth, not a soul understanding His heart. When I'm crying into a pillow, He is there because He wept tears of blood for the price He would soon have to pay. When my affections are fickle, He is there because He watched Peter's undying love turn to three denials.

His presence and understanding give me the uncanny ability to say three words that feel foreign and freeing on my tongue: *I forgive you*. I see Jesus hammered to the cross, the torture device His very own people placed Him on. And He said those beautiful words: "Father, forgive them, for they do not know what they are doing" (Luke 23:34 NIV).

Even in the statement, He offered grace, saying those people who knew what they were doing were misguided and messed up. He offered the forgiveness words after Pharisees wagged their mocking heads His way; a thief poked fun; a soldier offered vinegar. I cannot fathom a God who dared to leave perfection, to come to this pain-paved world and heal those who eventually screamed for His death.

And yet in the tiniest of ways, I can. Because I've been hurt by others before. I've felt abandoned. I've cut my feet on shards of glass others have laid before me. I have suffered directly because of others' sins (and as I write this, it agonizes me to say that others have suffered directly because of my myriad sins).

Oh, how we all need Jesus. Because He's been there, experiencing every facet of human joy, pain, anguish, revelation, neediness, exuberance, frailty—only He faced it all perfectly, wearing a countenance of forgiveness. He showed us how to experience God the Father in thin places: on mountaintops, in quiet moments, through the raging of days. I love Him for it.

8. Forgiveness Emboldens Your Prayers

RECENTLY THE LORD REMINDED ME OF AN ENEMY AND HOW MY PRAYING for her has morphed over the years. Here's my progression:

- Initially I was wholly David, invoking imprecatory prayers. (These are smiting-your-enemies types of prayers, where you ask God to deal swiftly with the person, exposing the sin, doling out swift justice.)
- Then by God's grace, I moved toward forgiveness prayers where I desperately longed to have a right heart, getting rid of my bitterness and learning to say, "I forgive her," again and again until it seemed to stick.
- Last, I moved toward blessing, where I asked the Lord to open her eyes, give her more of Himself, and bless her as she followed Him in her life.

So God reminded me of her again. Initially I ran through my process. Then I wondered whether she had done the same. Had she invoked imprecatory prayers upon me? Had she struggled to forgive me? Had she prayed for my blessing?

As I recounted, I asked God to listen to her prayers on my behalf, a scary move on my part. But here's how I worded it. Feel free to pray this prayer when you're concerned about someone who has hurt you or you have hurt:

> Jesus, if my friend has prayed vengeance upon me, I pray You would sift through the words and find the parts of me that need correction. No doubt there's a kernel of truth in the prayers. I am a sinner, in need of discipline and correction. Would you give the "enemy" in my life the holy gumption that he (she) needs to forgive me and let go of bitterness? And as I pray that, would You grant me the same request? And if my enemy dares to pray blessing over my life, please hear that prayer, and bless my enemy as I pray the same over his (her) life. Amen.

9. Forgiveness Can Change a Nation

THE MOST HUMBLING ACTS OF FORGIVENESS HAVE UTTERLY CHANGED the way I forgive. In reading about people who forgive the unforgivable, I suddenly feel small, the offenses against me petty in light of the atrocities in this crazy world.

Catherine Claire Larson wrote *As We Forgive: Stories of Reconciliation from Rwanda*—one of those life-changing books that will linger with me the rest of my life. It's not for the fainthearted. It's not for the hard-hearted or those bent toward stubborn unforgiveness. It's primarily a story of hope.

During one hundred days of 1994, there were 800,000 people brutally murdered in Rwanda—a genocide swifter in execution than Nazi gas chambers. Imagine the people of Denver and Colorado Springs—every man, woman, and child—suddenly gone from our population and you'll appreciate the scope of the horror. (And look at a map of Africa. Trace your finger due south of Uganda, due east of the Congo, and you'll appreciate the small size of this country.)[5]

Larson shares the stories of genocide survivors, recounting the unspeakable. But it does not stop there. She pulls back the curtain on the most ostentatious acts of forgiveness I've heard about, where genocide survivors choose to forgive those who perpetrated such violence. Together, through reconciliation practices and restorative justice, they are rebuilding their country from the ruins of hatred—all on the back of the One who still bears the scars for our sins today. Imagine a woman welcoming a man back into her life—the man who slaughtered her family. He must repay her by rebuilding her home. So he does. Her journey toward forgiving him is heart wrenching, but in the aftermath of such an act, I can barely keep my breath. She is Jesus in the situation. So utterly Jesus.

I came away from this book changed, deeply moved,

and inspired. Having seen the power of God help people forgive the seemingly unforgivable gave me hope that my wrestling with forgiveness would end in possible restoration. None of the forgiveness modeled was simple or easy or quickly won, nor does the book purport that reconciliation is merely forgiveness while forgetting. For true restoration to occur, the person perpetrating the atrocity must first fully own his or her sin and grieve it as such. And for the person who was sinned against to heal, he or she must revisit the place of grief.

All this dovetails beautifully into the message God's been birthing in me—to help people who suffer silently tell the truth about their pasts and choose the difficult path of forgiveness, in order to heal.

If God can reach into a genocide victim's heart and offer peace, if He can transform a murderer into a productive member of a reconciled society, then surely He can transform your pain today. That's the patent hope the gospel gives.

FORGIVENESS IS MULTILAYERED AND AMAZING. WE KNOW THAT. WE understand how hard it is to be a forgiving people. But what does it look like in real life? How can we live forgiveness? I'll end this chapter with an inspiring, gutsy story from my friends Chad and Sarah Markley. Several years ago, Sarah had an affair. Her journey back to Jesus and the heart of her husband has been difficult but amazing. And his story toward forgiveness and marital restoration should bring us all great hope. May this interview inspire you toward living a forgiveness lifestyle. We hear first from Chad, then Sarah.

CHAD, HOW DID YOUR UNDERSTANDING OF FORGIVENESS CHANGE IN the aftermath of learning about Sarah's affair?

> In the beginning, I did not want to forgive. The thing that really changed my perspective and heart was attending a screening of *The Passion of the Christ* the next day. When you are brooding, mad, and hurt, that is not the movie to watch. It broke me in half. When we left, I was still badly hurt, but it became very apparent to me what had been done for me on the cross, and I would not be forgiven if I didn't forgive. I guess it was a self-preservation thing at the heart. I didn't want God on my case like the king in the parable that forgave the guy a huge debt and then he runs out and puts a guy in prison who owed him fifty dollars. That parable kept running through my head that entire next week.

Did you think of yourself as a forgiving person before the affair?

> Yes. Growing up I was always the kid who would protect/defend the kid getting picked on. When someone

would hurt me, I would be quick to forgive, and when I was wrong I was always quick to repent and try to make it right. As I am older and more aware of myself and my feelings, I see that I've tended to be more forgiving of big things and apt to hold a grudge or get more hurt with smaller things. I can forgive infidelity but when you ignore me, I hold a grudge. Odd, I know. One thing to note: I was complicit in our lifestyle choices. I was wrapped up in pornography, and we were drinking and partying a lot. If I didn't start the fire, I certainly fanned the flames *a lot.*

What helped you move beyond the affair? What role did forgiveness play?

The parable above really pulled me through some of the valleys. Anything David wrote was hugely impactful in my life at the time. People had all kinds of things to share, but at the end of the day, most were stupid, and they had no idea. Our best traction was made in our professional marriage counseling sessions. Bottom line, pastors are not equipped to handle stuff like this and they shouldn't be expected to. This might sound overly simple, but we read through the Bible that year, four chapters each day. That one practice alone was the best thing for our relationship outside of professional counseling.

What is the greatest gift from that time in your marriage? How has that part of the story made your marriage better or stronger?

> We are stronger now because we know how much damage and heartbreak we can sustain. We got the crap kicked out of us when we screwed up. But by God's grace we didn't sink! We are stronger because we didn't give up, because we went all in and it worked.

What would you say to someone who has a hard time forgiving a spouse in a similar situation?

> I would say it isn't easy to forgive. God totally understands that, and He will labor with them through the process no matter how long it takes. I tell them what they experienced is not fair but that everything they have done to violate the relationship between them and their Creator also isn't fair. But that Christ saw fit to totally wipe all that clean, forgive them and bring them back like it never happened. I would tell them that people can change, and it's never too late to do so.

Sarah, how hard was it to come clean? What circumstances helped you decide to be honest?

> It was both difficult and easy. Difficult because I was laying it all out on the table. Telling the truth meant I had to be willing to give up all that we'd built (family, home, friends) in order to be right with God and Chad. But in a way there was ease to it, because I knew it was my only choice. Lying (like I had been) was killing me.

What did you expect Chad's reaction to be?

> I had no idea. I thought that he might take our daughter (she was two at the time), or that he wouldn't be able to really forgive me. In the back of my head (and heart) I hoped he would forgive. Even as far from good as we had walked, I knew him to be a person capable of sincere forgiveness. I was hoping for that, wishing for that. His initial reaction was not surprising to me: anger, bitterness, and fear. And then the brokenness in him that came soon after was a little surprising; I hadn't expected him to let God work in his heart so soon.

In a very real way, besides sinning against your husband, you sinned against yourself. How did you learn how to forgive yourself in the aftermath of what happened? Do you still struggle with forgiving yourself?

In all honesty this is something I still struggle with. For years I continued to apologize both to God and to Chad. Chad never brought it up again in any normal marital arguments that would follow, but in the back of my head I'd always wonder if he was thinking about it. I'm still seeing a counselor regularly, and together we are working through some of these issues. I think that forgiving oneself takes an incredible amount of self-assuredness that I think can only be found in Jesus. When we understand that we are truly grace-covered, then we can forgive ourselves with the strength that Jesus offers. I'm still working on it.

How has Chad's forgiveness helped you see yourself? What role does forgiveness play now in your relationship? (Obviously you both sin, and both have to extend it.)

It's interesting because I think that we have ease in forgiving larger transgressions, but that the minor, daily mishaps are the ones that catch us up. We can forgive huge mistakes but have difficulty extending grace for a messy kitchen. However, over the past nine years, we've learned a lot about grace and forgiveness. Chad's forgiveness has helped me to understand that I'm worthy of love, of grace, and of another chance to be who I was made to be.

To forgive as we've been forgiven makes for powerful stories and paves the way for surprising reconciliation. Although we can't force the kind of reconciliation that Chad and Sarah experienced, we can still live blessedly free by choosing to forgive those who hurt us. And when we do, we give others a clear picture of Jesus and the gospel.

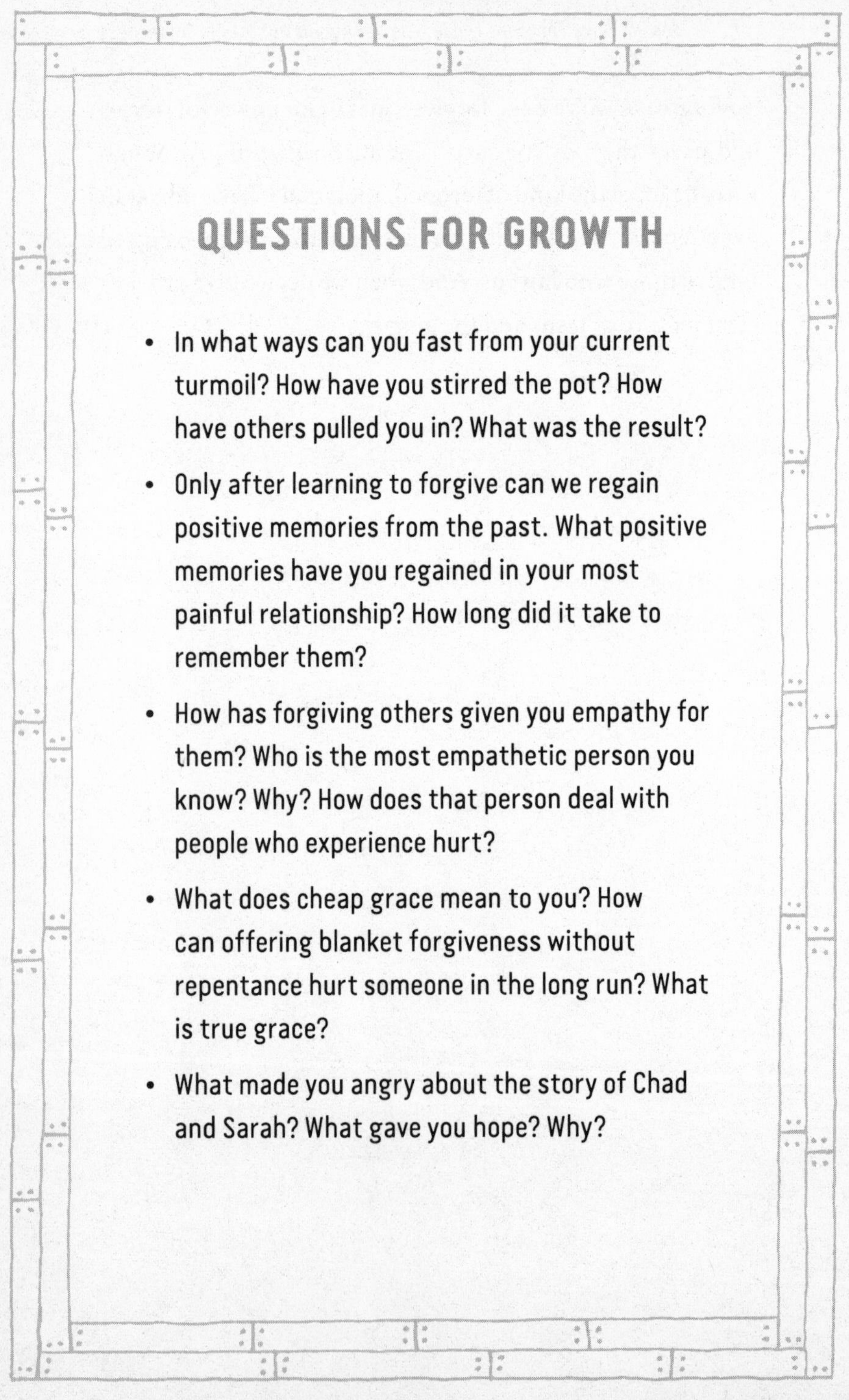

QUESTIONS FOR GROWTH

- In what ways can you fast from your current turmoil? How have you stirred the pot? How have others pulled you in? What was the result?
- Only after learning to forgive can we regain positive memories from the past. What positive memories have you regained in your most painful relationship? How long did it take to remember them?
- How has forgiving others given you empathy for them? Who is the most empathetic person you know? Why? How does that person deal with people who experience hurt?
- What does cheap grace mean to you? How can offering blanket forgiveness without repentance hurt someone in the long run? What is true grace?
- What made you angry about the story of Chad and Sarah? What gave you hope? Why?

"And Don't Let Us Yield to Temptation"

Dare to Engage Anyway

WHAT ARE YOU TEMPTED TO DO WHEN SOMEONE HURTS YOU? THE premise of this book is that pesky wall around your heart, the impenetrable fortress you vow to build higher and higher so no one can break in. When we're hurt, we protect. We wall off. We retreat. We leave. We falsely believe that life is too painful now, and leaving relationships will protect us from further pain. On one plane, this is true, but isolation rarely breeds joy or healing in the aftermath.

After one particular volatile interaction with a friend, the last thing I wanted to do was to go out of my way to meet more friends. I viewed people as potential mean girls, just waiting to find my weaknesses and skewer me with unkind words. So for a time, I lived in the land of blessed isolation. I kept myself aloof. In that loneliness I rehashed my friends' offenses, and they grew louder in my mind.

Only when I took baby steps toward new friends did I start to heal from the painful interactions. After I processed my angst with people who loved me, I found I could engage again, that not all people were bent on my demise.

How can the Lord's Prayer help us with the temptation to protect ourselves at any cost? When we first read this part of this prayer, we might be confused. Other translations read, "Lead us not into temptation" (NIV, KJV, ESV), which sounds as if God's job is to lead us there or He has a hand in the temptation. That's why I like the New Living Translation here, where it rightfully conveys the tone. God does not lead us toward temptation. James was very clear on that point: "When tempted, no one should say, 'God is tempting me.' For God cannot be tempted by evil, nor does he tempt anyone; but each person is tempted when they are dragged away by their own evil desire and enticed. Then, after desire has conceived, it gives birth to sin; and sin, when it is full-grown, gives birth to death" (James 1:13–15 NIV).

When we are hurt we are most vulnerable to give in to a variety of temptations—most of which cause us to isolate. In situations where life works well and people live in harmony with us, we aren't tempted to hurl anger someone's way. When life spins the way we want it to, we're not tempted to throw in the towel and court bitterness. But when friendships turn sour, when marriage falters, when enemies press in, that's when temptation looks seductive and right. It's when we're hard-pressed relationally that we give in to protectionism or panic. We're tempted to believe the worst or give up altogether. We build our cases, spending energy defending ourselves. We jump to conclusions. Sometimes we trust the wrong people in an effort to alleviate our pain. But the amazing thing is that God is always there, always beckoning upward to Him and outward to relationship. We don't have to be enslaved to fear.

Sometimes the Temptation Is to Fear

WHEN A CHRISTIAN LEADER BACKED ME INTO THE CORNER OF HER house, my children watching wide-eyed, I panicked inside. When her finger nearly touched my heart and her eyes flamed anger, I scooted away from the corner, grabbed my children, and got out of Dodge. For weeks, every time I saw this woman, I gave in to panic, my heart beating wildly, palms sweating, fear mounting. Fear became my autoresponder. It ruled me, escalated my pulse, and lumped my throat. It agonized my stomach and distorted my thinking. It got to the point that I couldn't function correctly if I thought she would be near. Panic defined the way I lived my life, and it prevented abundance and joy.

Eventually I realized that panic was no way to proceed. I couldn't live in fear for the rest of my life. Looking back on it, I recognize that fear had become a choice, which means I could've also chosen to give that fear to Jesus, ask for His help, and operate with faith toward Him instead of fear toward a person. It didn't occur to me that letting fear reign meant I was giving in to temptation.

Sometimes the Temptation Is to Believe the First Story You Hear

IT'S HAPPENED TO ME SO MANY TIMES THAT I HAVE A FEELING IT'S UNIversal. When we walk through hurt, whether our own or another's, we base our response on the first thing we hear. Proverbs asserts, "In a lawsuit the first to speak seems right, until someone comes forward and cross-examines" (Prov. 18:17 NIV).

Like when a friend talked about a person in a negative light, only to find out the story was wrong or at least not quite accurate. Yet I spent years believing this lie about a person, tempering the way I viewed her. Or the time someone detailed an elaborate conspiracy against her, only to find out later the story was fabricated.

There is power in the first story. We are tempted to believe that first story as gospel, then filter everything through that story.

But we shouldn't.

If we want to be mature believers growing beyond the pain inflicted by others, we need to exercise our discernment muscle. When others tell us something, we should be quiet, listen, then weigh the information. We shouldn't immediately take our friend's side, berating the other "awful" person. My husband and I have learned this lesson over the years as we've counseled married couples. I'll hear the wife's story and immediately form an impression of the husband. My husband will hear the husband's story and immediately form an impression of the wife. But when we're all together and the words fly, everyone's perceptions are wonky, and the truth lies somewhere between both stories.

Many years ago, a woman told me awful, awful things about someone else. I let them deter me from friendship for a time. But God told me to pursue that friendship. Although I did see that my first friend's words were often true, they were distorted. The woman didn't maliciously act the way she did; she lived in a very difficult situation and was doing what she knew in order to cope. If I had let the first story have the most power, I wouldn't have had the opportunity to speak into the second woman's life.

Here's the truth: we like to be right, especially about our opinions of other people. And we like to peddle our case against someone else to prove our point. We may have only half the story. And when we peddle destructive stories, we mar the potential of others to have meaningful relationships.

I'm not speaking here of wolves who parade around as sheep. We must warn about that. We have a moral obligation to protect others from predators. But we don't have a moral obligation to spread our stories because we want to be right, to appear to be the wronged ones.

I believe the first story far too often. Now I've become quieter, taking those first words to God, for Him to sift and weigh. And to pursue as God leads.

Sometimes the Temptation Is to Defend Ourselves

I'VE ALSO TAKEN UP MY CAUSE. I'VE LIVED FOR MICROMANAGING MY reputation, forgetting to let God be in control of that.

I'm finding the strength to let go of what people think of me. To let negative opinions (whether they are accurate or not) roll away from me.

Still, it's not easy. Especially when someone has a wrong opinion of me (or he or she chooses to believe the first story about me). I'd rather run around like a crazy woman letting everyone know that I'm not what he or she thinks of me, that my sum total is better, more laudable. But that only makes me look oddly guilty. And it expends energy I should be expending for Jesus and His kingdom. I wonder how much time I've wasted trying to be my own public relations manager when I should be serving others and letting opinions rest as they are.

I'm thankful that I've learned the beauty of silence. Jesus said not. one. word. before His accusers, when He certainly had a right to. His silence, no doubt, unnerved them. But He had such a well-connected heart to the Father that He knew He lived for the audience of One, not the audience of the crowd. Oh, to live like that!

A. B. Simpson put it beautifully:

> There is a place of stillness that allows God the opportunity to work for us and gives us peace. It is a stillness that

> ceases our scheming, self-vindication, and the search for a temporary means to an end through our own wisdom and judgment. Instead, it lets God provide an answer, through His unfailing and faithful love, to the cruel blow we have suffered.
>
> Oh, how often we thwart God's intervention on our behalf by taking up our own cause or by striking a blow in our own defense! May God grant each of us this silent power and submissive spirit.[1]

We shortchange God's great ability to defend us when we give in to the temptation to take up our cause. We thwart His redemptive purposes when we become our own little reputation saviors. And when we do, we forget to exercise faith. Instead of waiting on God for deliverance, we orchestrate our own.

David understood this. He saw God as his true defender, even when enemies were hell-bent on his destruction:

> *He reached down from heaven and rescued me;*
> *he drew me out of deep waters.*
> *He delivered me from my powerful enemies,*
> *from those who hated me and were too strong for me.*
> *They attacked me at a moment when I was in distress,*
> *but the Lord supported me.*
> *He led me to a place of safety;*
> *he rescued me because he delights in me.*
> *(2 Sam. 22:17–20)*

Sometimes the Temptation Is to Give Up

WHEN PEOPLE HURT US, WE'RE TEMPTED TO STOP TRYING, TO GIVE up, to lick our wounds and cease forward momentum. My friends faced this temptation when they moved to another country to relieve a couple who had pioneered a bed-and-breakfast for mission team workers.

Here is their story:

> A little over two years ago now we received a phone call asking if we wanted to come to another country to take over a ministry of housing and hosting short-term mission groups. My husband and I had been praying for some time about how we would enter the mission field. Then the call came. We prayed about it and sought godly counsel from our church's leadership. We accepted.
>
> In this acceptance there were two conditions: the biggest being we had to sell our house, and the second being the bed-and-breakfast needed to pay its own way. Unfortunately, it took a year and a half for God to sell our house in a depressed real estate market. So after a couple of yard sales and many tears, we left with our few possessions to be in full-time missions work. We let the caretakers know we'd be there in four days.
>
> We arrived at 3:00 a.m. with our stuff and our cats. Needless to say, we just went to sleep where we were told to sleep. When we got up the next morning, we discovered that no work had been done in preparation for our

arrival. The people who ran the mission station had not moved out. In addition, another person at the mission station met us with open hostility. Without knowing why, we'd become the enemy. We endured looks, harsh comments, and other derogatory behavior.

We spent the first week helping them (basically doing all the work to move them to their new home they had built in another location). We experienced several negative encounters—like open theft from one of the previous people, stories told about us and how bad we were, and a list of things too numerous to count.

This is not what we expected, especially since these people had invited us to come. We also walked into a place in total disrepair, dirty beyond belief, with leaking roofs and hardly any clients—meaning what they told us about the bed-and-breakfast paying its own way was not true.

Yet, in all of this, God's mercy rings true and is new every morning. If this weren't true, I would not have been able to get out of bed. Thankfully, things have changed greatly, and the biggest is the work that God did in my husband's and my hearts and in strengthening our walk with our heavenly Father. It is so true it is in adversity we learn to put feet to our faith and experience what it means to be one of God's kids. We get to have a true glimpse of how He loves us.

With that "homecoming," my missionary friends could've given up, repacked their belongings, and headed back to the

States. Though difficulties multiplied, they chose to persevere, even when the people who should've supported them became hostile and belligerent. When I think of their perseverance, I realize that anything worth doing in the kingdom is hard work. The enemy of our souls will do anything he can to thwart our mission, and his keenest tactic is using other Christians to discourage us.

Sometimes the Temptation Is to Misplace Our Trust

ODDLY, WHEN PEOPLE HURT US, WE FORGET THEIR WAYS AND JUMP right back into trust again. Maybe we hope that people can change, or perhaps we second-guess our perceptions from the last pain. Or maybe we're truly gluttons for punishment. We shouldn't grow so cynical that we wall ourselves off and never engage in relationships or community, but we must always reorient ourselves to this truth: people cannot ultimately satisfy us.

The psalmist put it succinctly:

> *Don't put your confidence in powerful people;*
> *there is no help for you there.*
> *When they breathe their last, they return to the earth,*
> *and all their plans die with them.*
> *But joyful are those who have the God of Israel as their helper,*
> *whose hope is in the Lord their God.* (Ps. 146:3–5)

God is the only Being we can really, truly, fully trust. He is the only One capable of filling up our hearts all the way. He exceeds our expectations by forgiving us, offering grace, and being near. His faithfulness shows us where our hierarchy of trust must be—first to Him, then to trustworthy people.

How should we respond when someone hurts us? How can we live beyond the temptations, conquering our fears? How can we respond to pain with grace and perseverance? King Hezekiah gave us a perfect example. He received a terrible diatribe about himself and the nation of Israel prior to possible invasion by Assyria. Not only did Sennacherib, the Assyrian leader, demean the people and their trust in God, but his words mocked God outright. Watch how Hezekiah responded, and notice how the structure of this prayer is a predecessor to the way that Jesus taught us to pray:

> After Hezekiah received the letter from the messengers and read it, he went up to the LORD's Temple and spread it out before the LORD. And Hezekiah prayed this prayer before the LORD: "O LORD, God of Israel, you are enthroned between the mighty cherubim! You alone are God of all the kingdoms of the earth. You alone created the heavens and the earth. Bend down, O LORD, and listen! Open your eyes, O LORD, and see! Listen to Sennacherib's words of defiance against the living God. It is true, LORD, that the kings of Assyria have destroyed all these nations. And they have thrown the gods of these nations into the fire and burned them. But

> of course the Assyrians could destroy them! They were not gods at all—only idols of wood and stone shaped by human hands. Now, O Lord our God, rescue us from his power; then all the kingdoms of the earth will know that you alone, O Lord, are God." (2 Kings 19:14–19)

Hezekiah remembered who God was and reminded himself of who he needed to be in the situation. Without the Lord's intervention, Hezekiah knew he would be doomed. So he spread out his complaints and requests before God. Honesty surged through his words. What I love about his petition is his zeal for God's reputation alone. And his foresight to see that every trial is meant for God's glory and fame.

When we're tempted in the midst of a painful relationship, we're prone to seek our comfort, control, and reputation. But mature believers do the opposite. We ask for God's will to be done, for Him to take divine note of the situation and act on our behalf for the sake of His name, not ours.

The temptation is always to build our kingdom, to raise our flag, to herald our agenda, to prove our rightness. But the Jesus way is to pray as He did, and in that, we find deeper growth, greater peace, and stronger faith. In Jesus, we have a sure place to put our pain and the strength to risk again. He heals us enough so we're no longer afraid to befriend more people. He forgives us when we build walls, and He understands the pain of betrayal in such a way that He can perfectly come alongside us. When we plead with Him to help us resist temptation, we partner with Him in relationship. Because He blesses us with relationship with Him, He enables us to move through our painful friendships and live openhearted.

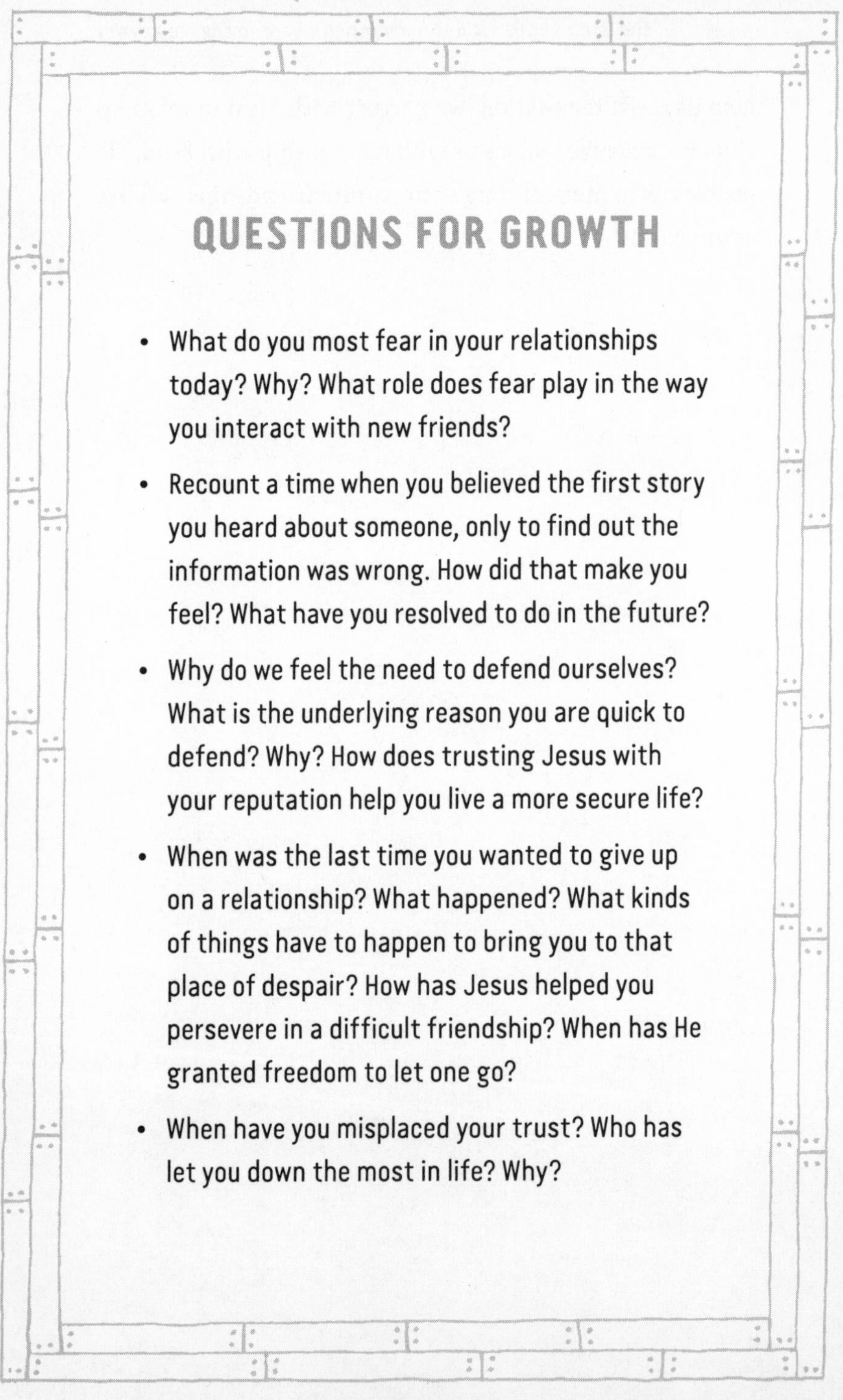

QUESTIONS FOR GROWTH

- What do you most fear in your relationships today? Why? What role does fear play in the way you interact with new friends?
- Recount a time when you believed the first story you heard about someone, only to find out the information was wrong. How did that make you feel? What have you resolved to do in the future?
- Why do we feel the need to defend ourselves? What is the underlying reason you are quick to defend? Why? How does trusting Jesus with your reputation help you live a more secure life?
- When was the last time you wanted to give up on a relationship? What happened? What kinds of things have to happen to bring you to that place of despair? How has Jesus helped you persevere in a difficult friendship? When has He granted freedom to let one go?
- When have you misplaced your trust? Who has let you down the most in life? Why?

"But Rescue Us from the Evil One"

Be Fully Alive

THE ENEMY OF OUR SOULS WANTS TO DO US HARM. HE WANTS TO steal, kill, and destroy us (John 10:10). His deepest intention is to separate us from God, then from others. He attacks at the core message of the gospel that Jesus delineated. When a religious leader asked, "'Teacher, which is the greatest commandment in the Law?' Jesus replied: 'Love the Lord your God with all your heart and with all your soul and with all your mind.' This is the first and greatest commandment. And the second is like it: 'Love your neighbor as yourself.' All the Law and the Prophets hang on these two commandments" (Matt. 22:36–40 NIV).

If Satan can cause us to question God, to believe He

is not good, he's won a giant battle. And if he can't create that kind of wedge, he gleefully delights in doing the next best thing: alienating us from others. That wall around your heart that you've cherished, protected, and rebuilt after each offense doesn't hurt others as much as it hurts you. It separates you from God, even though you might reason that walling yourself off doesn't have anything to do with your view of God.

Jesus didn't separate the two. Love God. Love others. They're intertwined, forever linked. You can't have one without the other.

So when Jesus asked us to pray, "Rescue us from the evil one," He wasn't simply asking us to refrain from sinful behavior (though that's part of it). He charged us to live a fully alive life, openhearted, willing to love others even when there's a strong possibility we'll be hurt again. He asked us to do only what He did on this earth. He loved God passionately, and He loved those people who spat in His face.

The measure of how well we truly love God is how well we love others. I don't much like that because I'd rather retreat and say, "I love You, God," in the quiet of my home, while keeping pesky relationships at a safe distance. This works for a period of time, but it's not healthy. Without people I'm safe, but I'm not sweet. I'm not vulnerable. I can give in easily to my selfishness if there aren't others to worry about. Sure, my heart is protected, but for what purpose? To live alone and stingy the rest of my life?

Today I write this in isolation, thankful for a respite. But

I write with restlessness, a longing for significance. And significance can't happen without other people. I need them. They need me. And God wants all of us to love others—He built us for adventurous impact. Where would Mother Teresa have been without people in her life? Would she have made such an impact on the world if she walled off her heart from others? The truth is, people who influence this world have learned the secret of connecting with others. They've not let Satan trick them into stoic isolation.

Easy to write but not easy to live.

When we pray, "Rescue us from the evil one," we put ourselves on the battlefront where we risk getting hurt again. We allow God access to the walls around our hearts, daring to declare, "Take down the bricks, whatever it takes." We usher in a new life, an openhearted way of relating to people that expands the kingdom of God.

I know you're afraid. But you need not be. Jesus is bigger than any pain someone can inflict. But we live as if that's not true. We live as if Jesus is smaller than the pain, which is why we no longer trust Him to protect our hearts.

I'm not saying we should be foolish people who run helter-skelter into damaging relationships. We are told to guard our hearts (Prov. 4:23). The whole book of Proverbs instructs us to be wise in the way we deal with fools and perpetrators. The thrust of Jesus' desire for us is to be open enough to risk, to no longer view relationships as potential pain, to love Him enough to give Him the hurt that may materialize in relationships.

One story may help.

When I met her, I had no idea she'd become a foe. She exuded life and laughter and friendship, and we became swift friends. I entrusted my soul to her, telling her girlfriend things, secrets, and the joys that I seldom shared with others. She let me bear her burdens, and she reciprocated conversations. She praised me, and I praised her. We connected over lunches, tea, worship, family, and long, leisurely dinners. I thought so many good things about my friend; I savored her friendship and adored her company.

And yet there was this little niggling I kept shoving back down. This small knowing that something wasn't quite right. Whenever I'd bring up Jesus, she'd balk, which was odd because she claimed to love Him. When I pressed her about growth, her eyes averted. And she often expressed off-kilter views of God, embracing only what she perceived as His grace-filled parts and shunning any mention of His holiness or the requirements for full lifestyle discipleship.

She played her part well, that of a friend who seemed to like Jesus a lot, but later proved to be an enemy of Him and me.

When things soured and I crossed an invisible line that turned her against me, I felt the venom in an instant. Have you ever had that happen? A friend morphs to enemy, but that betrayal catches you by the throat? Surprises you in every possible way?

She sent virulent words, the kind that splay you out, make you question everything. I felt smaller than the type on this page in the aftermath of her stinging paragraphs. It took me a long time to realize that there are people in this world who pretend, play a role, and are so caught by Satan's traps and tactics that they recoil and act on his behalf. Receiving those e-mails also convicted me of some of the diatribes I've sent and immediately regretted. It's sad to say that I have been one of those people who have hurt others with harsh words. This realization makes me humble, and it helps me to see her e-mails as a cautionary tale—to not hit SEND next time I'm angry and want to prove a point by demeaning someone.

Instead of letting this angry friend define the way I interacted with new friends, I had to learn to give the pain to Jesus. I had to remind myself that our battle isn't against people. The problem comes when we mistake our friends and enemies for Satan and think our battle is against them. It's not.

Jesus concluded this amazing prayer with these words: "But rescue us from the evil one." He didn't ask that we be rescued from people. In fact, He prayed this in His High Priestly prayer: "I am coming to you now, but I say these things while I am still in the world, so that they may have the full measure of my joy within them. I have given them your word and the world has hated them, for they are not of the world any more than I am of the world. My prayer is not that you take them out of the world but that you protect them from the evil one" (John 17:13–15 NIV).

So on this earth we will have relational discord. It's a known fact. We won't be rescued from it. But Jesus promised that He will rescue us from the evil one. This good news squares with our experience. I used to think that when I met Jesus, all my pain would magically dissipate, all my relationships would rise up and bless me, and from henceforth, all would be peachy.

That belief lasted about an hour as I rode home from the weekend camp where I met Jesus when I was fifteen years old. Full of zeal and joy and hope, I determined to share Jesus with my unsuspecting mother. But instead of responding with butterflies and daffodils, her reaction tended more toward angry fireworks. She accused me of being in a cult. I pleaded with her to ask Jesus to come into her heart, but she refused.

"So what happens when you die?" I asked with as much evangelical gumption as I could muster.

"When I die, I'm dead," she said, confirming her nihilistic view of the afterlife.

I cried, pleaded, and cried some more, retreating to my room. From that moment in time, my mom and I have not seen eye-to-eye in eternal matters. I continue to pray that the Lord will woo her to Himself, though at times this prayer feels like it's getting nowhere. It's hard when a parent acts as an enemy to your faith.

And it's hard when anyone acts that way. It's enough to make you want to live reserved, keeping your passions close to the chest, singing safely behind that wall.

How do we find victory? How can we joyfully risk even when it's excruciating to do so? The secret lies in our responses when people hurt us. We'll be tempted to rail, retaliate, ignore, or even pretend that the painful words don't hurt. But that's not openhearted living. Living without walls means we become proactive in the way we deal with hurt. Here are some ways we can joyfully escape Satan's relational traps:

Let Go of Busyness

I WONDER HOW MUCH RELATIONAL STRESS WE COULD SOLVE BY being available. Our lives are so busy that we often gloss over small annoyances and let discord build up over time, only to have blowups and blowouts every few months. Truth be told, no one who is overworked and stressed out is good at relationships. Satan knows this and dangles overactivity in front of us like a tempting charm. After all, if we busy ourselves, we won't have to deal with our friendship issues. We won't have to fight (in a positive way) for our family relationships. We can avoid instead.

Escape this trap by choosing sabbath, by building margin into your life.[1]

Make Room for Possible Fake Christians

AS I MENTIONED IN THE STORY AT THE BEGINNING OF THIS CHAPTER, sometimes people pretend to be Christians. Having people like that hurt us sends us down an existential path of stress. Although it is true that Christ followers will hurt us, sometimes it helps to reevaluate whether they truly follow Christ. Of course it isn't something you say out loud or proclaim.

It's something you keep to yourself. Only God can judge a person's heart. But letting it be a possibility that the person hurting you isn't walking with God takes a bit of the sting out. People who don't yet know Jesus can't help acting in an unchristian manner.

Escape this trap by offering grace to those who hurt you.

Calm Yourself

ANOTHER TRAP WE FACE IS THE OVERREACTION TRAP. SOMEONE tells us something we don't want to hear (and it may be right!), and we choose to overreact. We amplify the initial sin by yelling our response. Proverbs 10:19 warns, "Too much talk leads to sin. Be sensible and keep your mouth shut." One of the most interesting things I've learned about great relationships: the best predictability of a marriage's healthy survival or demise is whether the spouses assume positive intent toward each other. In other words, they don't jump to negative conclusions when they initially encounter a problem. This isn't an easy discipline to cultivate, particularly in our pessimistic, quick-to-blame culture.

Escape this trap by keeping your mouth shut.

Find Others

PERHAPS THE MOST INSIDIOUS TRAP IS THIS: SATAN KNOWS THAT we grow best in community, so he'll do everything he can to undermine our desire to be in it. He'll whisper about how much easier it would be if we'd just stay hermits. He'll remind us that relationships are messy and they're just not worth enmeshing ourselves in. While it is true that relationships breed mess, it's also true that without them we'll wither into ourselves. Proverbs 14:4 reminds us, "Without oxen a stable stays clean, but you need a strong ox for a large harvest." If we withdraw and isolate, our lives (stables) stay clean of the mess of people. But we shortchange our growth if we don't welcome them back in.

Escape this trap by anticipating the inevitable mess of relationships.

Don't Give Up

SOMETIMES WHEN OTHERS HURT US, AND IT HAPPENS MORE THAN WE think we can bear, we want to give up. The temptation to throw in the relational towel is strong. The problem is, we usually do this when we rely on our own strength. We forget that God's greatest strength shows up in our weakness. A friend tweeted this recently: "I've heard it said that in walking through grief, you don't realize you are turning a corner toward healing until after you've rounded the bend."

When we give up too soon, we can't see the healing path or discern the new vista that God brings to us. And if we fully give in to fatalism, we'll conclude, "Everyone hurts me, so I won't open myself up to people again." This may be a safe response, but it's not a good one. The absolute best blessings in my life have come on the other side of grief, after patient endurance. James encouraged us, "Let it [endurance] grow, for when your endurance is fully developed, you will be perfect and complete, needing nothing" (James 1:4).

Escape this trap by choosing to endure and asking for God's strength when you can't persist in your own strength.

Realize You're Not the Only One

SATAN LIKES YOU TO BELIEVE THAT YOU ARE THE ONLY ONE WITH this problem, the only one who has been hurt in this specific way by that person. All of us have unique pains and a tapestry of difficult relationships, yet we do not exclusively suffer. Our pain is not unique. In fact, all of us are in the same relational *Titanic,* sinking because of the iceberg of barbs and rejection. God promises us comfort, not just for our sake, but so that we can come alongside others who also feel like their pain is uniquely theirs. We become a part of God's great healing plan. He heals us so we can point others to His healing. All together, we realize we're not alone in our suffering. God takes the very thing we think will break us and transforms that pain so others won't feel alone.

Escape this trap by daring to look first to God for healing, then directing that healing toward others who suffer.

Understand That the World Isn't Against You

LIFE IS TOO SHORT TO BE AT WAR WITH EVERYONE. AND THE TRUTH IS, you're not at odds with every single human being on the planet. When a heap of painful relationships bombards us, our tendency is to think catastrophically, not realistically. We say things like, "No one wants to be my friend," or "Everyone is opposing me." At that point we have to take a moment to go to a quiet place, settle our souls, and ask Jesus to encourage us. We need to read Scripture to remind us of the truth that even if we feel everyone is against us, God is for us. Remember that this life exists in seasons. There are times when our relationships seem to sing symphonies, other times when we feel blah about our friendships, and still others when every relationship feels prickly. That's okay. Things will change, but the great constant is God's constant care for us.

Escape this trap by quieting yourself and asking God for His encouragement.

Accept That This Pain Doesn't Define You Forever

ANOTHER TRAP IS THINKING, *THIS BLOWUP/ISSUE/PROBLEM WILL define me the rest of my life. I will always fail at relationships. I'll never grow beyond this.* If we choose to believe these lies, we'll never overcome our hurt. We'll circle back around, stepping back into the same messes. The truth? God is in the great redemption business. He delights in taking people who fail in relationships and making them whole, happy, and engaging. There is hope for you. As long as you are breathing and the Holy Spirit resides in you, you can change. Other people may not change. You can't control them after all. But you have the power to change your response if you lean on Jesus. You don't have to remain bitter for a lifetime.

Escape this trap by defining yourself by the Lord's redemption, not your failure.

Recognize That It's Never Always Their Fault

PERHAPS THE BIGGEST TRAP WE FALL INTO IS POINTING AN ACCUSING finger at everybody else, determining that our problems are always because of others. If we never accept blame or look at ourselves and discern our faults, we'll continue to make the same mistakes again and again. Such people always wonder why they fail in the same way in every relationship. Surprise: they are the constant! To truly move forward, we must be a repentant people, willing to see our sin and offering it up to Jesus with sorrow.

Escape this trap by practicing repentance in your relationships.

Trust This Trial Will Enhance Your Growth Story

SATAN WHISPERS THIS LIE IN YOUR EAR: "GOD ASKS TOO MUCH OF you." You welcome his words, not realizing it's a poisonous trap. The truth is, God asks just the right amount of you so that you will grow stronger and deeper and wider. Paul told of a time he nearly died, yet God used this extreme stretching to once again prove He is big and capable:

> We do not want you to be uninformed, brothers and sisters, about the troubles we experienced in the province of Asia. We were under great pressure, far beyond our ability to endure, so that we despaired of life itself. Indeed, we felt we had received the sentence of death. But this happened that we might not rely on ourselves but on God, who raises the dead. He has delivered us from such a deadly peril, and he will deliver us again. On him we have set our hope that he will continue to deliver us. (2 Cor. 1:8–10 NIV)

God often stretches you beyond your comfort to grow you. Relationships are His invitation for growth and trust. If you can't trust Him as you try a new relationship, what does that say about your trust level? Is God bigger than your hurt?

Escape this trap by knowing God will bring good from this trial, no matter how hard it is.

ALTHOUGH IT MAY BE HARD TO BELIEVE THAT WE HAVE A LURKING enemy who intends to overthrow us with his evil plans, it's not hard to see evil in this world. Unfortunately much of that evil comes through others, which makes it hard to process and move on. The end of this prayer is a holy reminder, a warning—that every day we are in a battle where the health of our souls is at stake. Daily we pray to be delivered from the evil one, no matter how he or his minions manifest themselves, particularly in our relationships.

The good news? God is a relational God, and He is on our side. He understands the heartache that comes from painful relationships. He walked the earth, our earth, His feet touching the soil we touch. He experienced everything the Devil threw at him, and He did so at His most vulnerable moment—being half-starved, alone, and in the wilderness. Consider Him! Believe Him! Trust Him! The author of Hebrews reminded us, "Consider him who endured such opposition from sinners, so that you will not grow weary and lose heart" (Heb. 12:3 NIV).

The Devil wins (though he cannot ultimately win) when we give in to relational weariness and build a wall. Instead, let's remember Jesus, who authored this prayer, who triumphed over evil, who forgave those who hurt and betrayed Him, who helped the oppressed. Jesus loves to come to our aid when we feel buried beneath the weight of relational pain. He is available. He will bring about His purposes in us. He will heal us from pain-inflicted words.

The amen to this prayer is ultimately a heroic triumph, found from the strength, power, and life of Jesus. On that cross where the Devil danced his short-lived victory, Jesus conquered him through death, then raucous resurrection. What looked like the defeat of God spelled ultimate defeat to Satan.

It is possible to live an openhearted life. At the beginning of this chapter, I referenced John 10:10. Let's look at it in context: "I tell you the truth, I am the gate for the sheep. All who came before me were thieves and robbers. But the true sheep did not listen to them. Yes, I am the gate. Those who come in through me will be saved. They will come and go freely and will find good pastures. The thief's purpose is to steal and kill and destroy. My purpose is to give them a rich and satisfying life" (John 10:7–10). If you have a wall firmly built around your heart, ask Jesus, the great gateway, to make a doorway through. He can. He is the gate. He is the avenue leading toward a rich and satisfying life—not a stingy, walled-off life.

What do you want your life to be? When you're near death, will you herald the times you safely kept yourself from the hearts of others? Will you smile in satisfaction that so few people hurt you? Is that the measure of an abundant life?

Life is hard. People are sometimes mean and petty and awful. But they're also amazing and beautiful and sacrificial. You'll miss the latter if you wall yourself off from the former. Our Good Shepherd knows this. He is a gentle shepherd, though. He won't bulldoze your wall if you don't want Him to. He won't make you *like* people. But He provided you with His life as a holy example of openhearted living. And He promises that you won't know the strength of God unless you acknowledge your weakness.

We are afraid of others, but Jesus is not. He created them.

We don't want to hurt. Jesus didn't either. He asked the Father to take away the cross, but ultimately He faced it. If He can do that, He can come alongside us when others cross us.

We don't want to risk yet again, but Jesus daily risks with every human on this earth, wooing people to Himself, though they've built walls against Him.

We are weary. Jesus was too. He loved this entire human race, all who sinned like crazy against Him and nailed Him to the cross. Yet His love persisted.

We can't tear down our walls. Jesus knows how. He built us. He knows the way we protect ourselves. And He shoulders our pain as if it were His own.

We'd rather nurse bitterness. But Jesus beckons us to sacrifice and growth and risk. His life exemplified all three.

In short, we can't, but He can. He can hold our hands when we're tired of all the pain. He can take that pain, grow us, and give us perspective later. He will teach us lessons we'd never learn in isolation and enlarge our hearts accordingly. He will change the world through us if we dare let Him.

And in that, there's victory—over our enemy, Satan. Over the callousness of our hearts. Over tightfisted living.

What life do you want? A walled-off one? Or a rich and satisfying one?

I hope you choose the second.

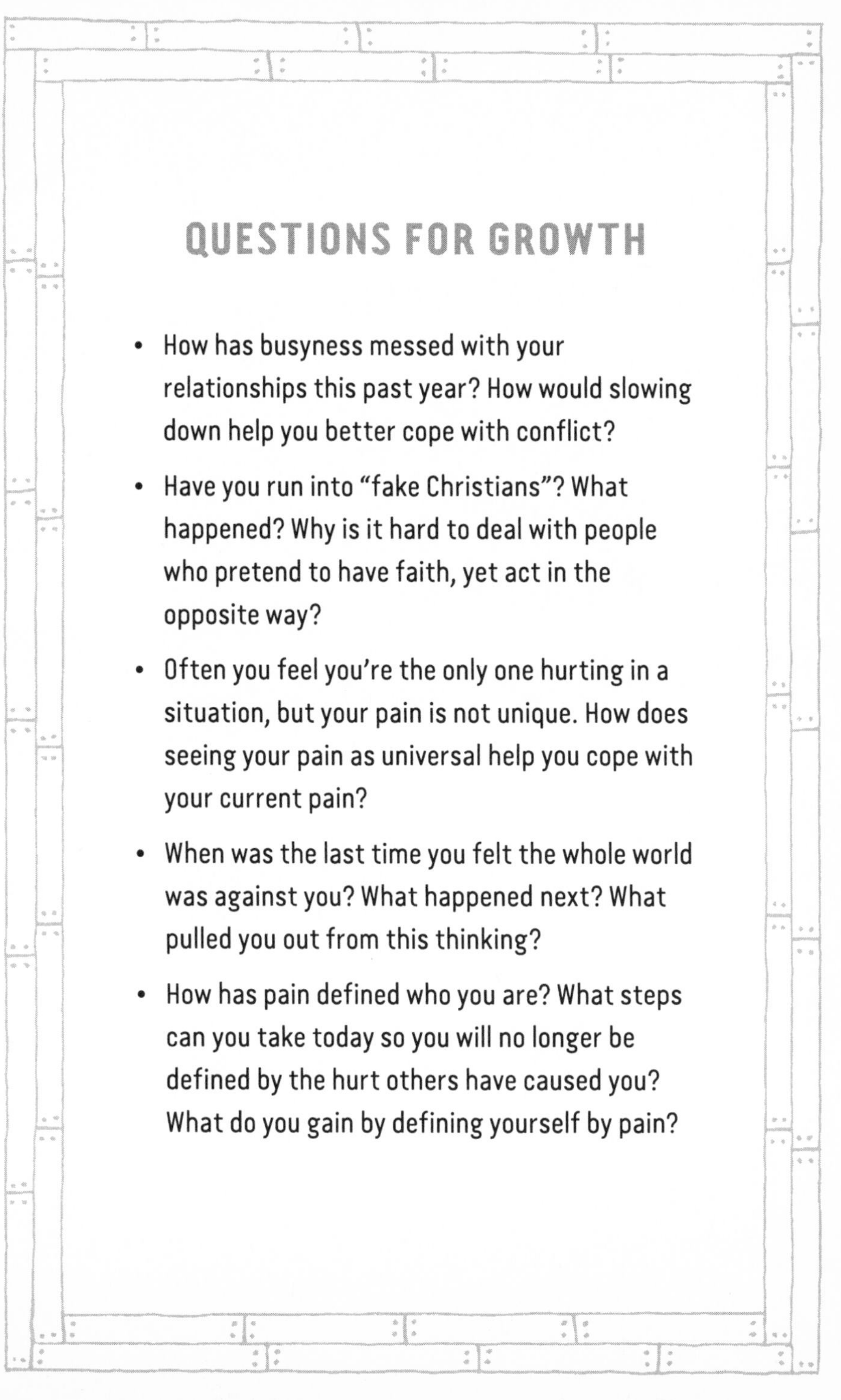

QUESTIONS FOR GROWTH

- How has busyness messed with your relationships this past year? How would slowing down help you better cope with conflict?
- Have you run into "fake Christians"? What happened? Why is it hard to deal with people who pretend to have faith, yet act in the opposite way?
- Often you feel you're the only one hurting in a situation, but your pain is not unique. How does seeing your pain as universal help you cope with your current pain?
- When was the last time you felt the whole world was against you? What happened next? What pulled you out from this thinking?
- How has pain defined who you are? What steps can you take today so you will no longer be defined by the hurt others have caused you? What do you gain by defining yourself by pain?

Epilogue

An Open Heart

WE'VE BEEN ON A JOURNEY TOGETHER, WALKING THROUGH THIS amazing prayer, learning about relationships, and dealing with pain. We've seen the devastation that walls produce in our lives. And I hope we've left the pages of this book with a longing—to trust Jesus with our pain, to believe He alone can protect our hearts, to risk again in relationships not for our sake but for His. To love openhearted and free.

As we finish, I want to give you a gift. He's not really mine to give; He's His to give. Jesus.

When I walked through one of the most painful encounters in my life, my friend's words cut through me.

Though I really hadn't wanted to talk to her about her angry responses to others, God pressed me to.

"Instead of reacting with anger," I said, "why not be

offended and let it lie there? Why not be like Jesus and forgive instead of retaliate?"

Leveling her eyes to mine, she said, "No one is like Jesus." She insinuated that what I asked was impossible, too lofty, unattainable.

And she was right.

There's only one Jesus, and not one of us is Him.

But we'll miss out on freedom, joy, forgiveness, love, and tenderness if we fail to grasp at Jesus. The great beauty of the Christian life isn't our ability to live it, to form an elaborate façade of having it all together; it's our weakness that welcomes His strength within us. Read J. B. Phillips's translation of 2 Corinthians 12:9–10: "'My grace is enough for you: for where there is weakness, my power is shown the more completely.' Therefore, I have cheerfully made up my mind to be proud of my weaknesses, because they mean a deeper experience of the power of Christ. I can even enjoy weaknesses, suffering, privations, persecutions and difficulties for Christ's sake. For my very weakness makes me strong in him."

We don't have to be awesome. Jesus does.

We don't have to know how to be strong after someone has hurt us. Jesus knows how. He modeled that kind of holy resilience in His life and on the cross.

We don't have to give in to bitterness. Of all the people on this crazy earth, He had the most reasons to be bitter. The entire human race imputed its sin to Him, gave Him its worst. And He bore that sin because of the "joy set before Him" (Heb. 12:2 NASB).

We don't have to wear relational devastation as a badge, letting it affect us the rest of our lives. Jesus bears the sin against us, the sin we commit in the aftermath. Ours is an act of beautiful and painful relinquishment. He is best equipped to bear all the pain.

We don't have to walk around with a chip on our souls. Jesus heals. He does. He will. We need to be willing.

Our gift to Him isn't our ability; it's our inability. It's our weakness, our surrender. Our letting go of micromanaging our lives and controlling others' lives and giving Jesus full control. After all, He is God, and we are not.

And how do we do that? Simple. By kneeling. By praying. By hollering and whimpering our needs, wants, pains, bewilderments to Jesus. That's the safest place to be, knees to the earth, hearts bowed and broken, in a position of humbleness and readiness.

We find the treasures of an openhearted life in the Lord's Prayer, in that position of petition. Next time you recite the prayer, let its words wash over your painful interactions from the last week. Allow it to remind you of Jesus' nearness to your pain and His ability to shoulder it. Recall the subtitles of each chapter as they follow the ancient words:

Pray first.

Live in your Father's affection.

Allow God to be God.

Walk in the Great Right Now.

Respond like Jesus.

Let heaven frame your relationships.

Ask Jesus for help.

Be repentant.

Defy bitterness.

Dare to engage anyway.

Be fully alive.

Amen!

I'm excited for you. Deeply so. Because I know that if you catch the privilege it is to kneel your life this way, fully surrendered to our powerful, amazing God, your life will never, ever be the same. You'll be ruined for the mundane. The walls that kept you safe from others will implode, opening your heart to beautiful heartache. You'll no longer be content with living in reaction to the pain that others inflict. Instead, you'll ask for healing, then seek to be an agent of healing. You'll witness your pain transform into a desire to see God's kingdom expand. People will seek you out, not because you're awesome but because God is.

In this wall-abolishing adventure, I wish you an open-hearted life.

ACKNOWLEDGMENTS

I'VE WRITTEN A LOT OF THESE PARAGRAPHS ABOUT WHAT I'M GRATEful for and who has deeply blessed me as I've written my books. This time I want to do something a little different. This book is about relationships. About people and hurt and joy.

Every time I write a book, I worry a little that God will cause me to go through a trial related to the book's contents. Imagine my fear when I wrote about spiritual warfare, or my hesitation when I wrote the book *Everything*.

And truth be told, God did take me on an "everything" journey this year. Right before the book released, our youngest daughter had scary hospital-worthy symptoms (she is since better, alleluia). Our finances shimmied. My career felt wrecked. So many other stressful circumstances vied for my attention, so much so that I felt I needed a break from my life. Have you ever felt that way? Jesus remained, but everything else seemed to crumble.

Everything, that is, except my relationships. We're in a healthy place, joyful in a great church. I have significant friendships and incredible support. But as *The Wall Around Your Heart* births, I'm painfully aware of one relationship that has crumbled. A longtime friend and I experienced a rift that breaks my heart. In those places of heartache and why, I've only been able to settle myself by reimagining our relationship fully whole on heaven's shores.

So I acknowledge this friend and pray for restoration. The seeming demise of a friendship keeps me close to Jesus, and it reminds me to pray for you, the reader, as you battle your own relational minefields. This stuff is hard, folks. But you are brave to hold and read this book.

To my prayer team, I cannot, cannot, cannot express my gratitude enough. If I could I'd send you all Lindt dark chocolate for life. I love you. I need you. I'm grateful for our near-decade of togetherness. Big hugs to Twilla, Renee, Carla, Caroline, Cheramy, Jeanne, D'Ann, Dorian, Erin, Ginger, Helen, Holly, Jen, Kathy, Katy G., Katy R., Denise, Anita, Diane, Cyndi, Lesley, Leslie, Liz, Marcia, Marion, Marybeth, Pam, Paula, Phyllis, Becky, Sandi, Sarah, Tim, Tina, Tracy, John, Nicole, Tosca, Marilyn, TJ, Patrick, Jody, Susan, Ariel, Mary, Amy, Lisa, Dena, Carol, Kathryn, Esther, Susie, Christy, Kimberly, Jodi, Ericka, Denise, Alice, Randy, Paul, Jan, Sophie, Sarah, Michele, Judy, Thomas, Heidi, Aldyth, and Sue.

To the DeMuth Advisory Board, thank you for walking me through this "everything" year. You've been a huge source of wisdom and steadiness. Thanks to Patrick, Pam, Thomas, Randy, Alice, Heidi, Kimberly, Denise, Holly, Leslie, D'Ann, Jody, Cathleen, Esther, and Sandi.

A huge rah-rah-rah to my cheerleaders: my agent, Esther Fedorkevich, and my editor, Bryan Norman. The synergy of the three of us changed my life. Thanks, too, to the awesome folk at Thomas Nelson who are championing this book: Janene MacIvor, Kimberly Boyer, and Chad Cannon.

To my dear family, Patrick, Sophie, Julia, and Aidan, you represent the best relationships in my life, and the reason why I fight to keep an open, wall-free heart. I love you.

Jesus, thank You for tearing down the walls, even when I'd rather barricade myself cocooned inside. I'd rather live with pain and engagement than isolation and safety. Let the adventure continue!

Appendix

Dealing with Wolves

PERHAPS ONE OF THE MOST DAMAGING HEARTACHES WE FACE AS believers in Jesus is finding out the people we thought were Christian leaders instead acted as wolves in shepherds' clothing. Jesus warned His disciples on more than one occasion to be on the lookout for such people: "Watch out for false prophets. They come to you in sheep's clothing, but inwardly they are ferocious wolves" (Matt. 7:15 NIV); and "I am sending you out like sheep among wolves. Therefore be as shrewd as snakes and as innocent as doves" (Matt. 10:16 NIV). And the apostle Paul issued a similar warning: "I know that after I leave, savage wolves will come in among you and will not spare the flock" (Acts 20:29 NIV).

Wolves aren't nice, particularly when they're wearing wool. They look kind, but underneath, they growl.

And sometimes wolves make their ways into our churches. Notice that Paul said they'd be "among you." This fact makes our recovery from their abuse that much harder because we can't believe that kind of betrayal happens at the hands of Christian leaders.

Another issue that trips us up and the Enemy uses to sideline us is abusive leadership in ministries and churches. This topic has been ricocheting in my heart and head many years. Although I'm thankful I haven't had an extreme experience with spiritual abuse, some incidents have made me leery of churches and ministries that bully. In the aftermath of those incidents, I've practically smelled the sulfurous breath of the Enemy, and I've let each interaction with abusive ministries sour me toward church and ministry.

A leader told me that even though I was burned out and losing my health, I had to stay in the ministry because if I didn't, I would lose all my gifting to do future ministry. One church's common message was that it had the corner on the market of Jesus and if we ventured elsewhere, we would miss God's highest for us. One leader we met used ministry as a vehicle for his great gain, lying to and manipulating donors so that he could earn more and more money. One ministry shamed me into throwing away all my evil music (including Lionel Richie and Duran Duran . . . oh, the evil!). One leader believed that allowing evil to continue in a church was fine, ignoring the victims and preferring the perpetrators.

I have friends who share hard stories too—one forced

out of ministry because she dared to bring up excesses and character issues; another who was ridiculed, then dismissed for insinuating an affair was brewing within the leadership, only to find out he'd been right all along. I know a woman subjected to verbal abuse by a mentor in ministry, immobilizing her from professionally speaking for a year because of it.

Since you're reading this book, I imagine you have a story or two to tell.

In taking all these stories into my heart, I've discovered ten traits of spiritually abusive ministries and churches. This list is not exhaustive, but it typifies what happens. Often you don't realize you're in an abusive ministry situation until your health is damaged, your soul is torn, or your non-church relationships suffer. My heart in sharing this list is to shed light on unhealthy, manipulative, controlling practices so that you can see what the enemy is up to, how he stirs up trouble even within our churches and ministry structures.

1. They Have a Distorted View of Respect

ABUSIVE PEOPLE FORGET THE SIMPLE ADAGE THAT RESPECT IS earned, not granted. Leaders in this paradigm demand respect without having earned it by good, honest living. They get angriest when people don't dare to show them proper respect, and they use this "lack of respect" as grounds for shunning members or humiliating them into submission.

2. They Demand Personal Allegiance as Proof of the Follower's Allegiance to Christ

IT'S EITHER HIS OR HER WAY TO FOLLOW JESUS OR NO WAY. AND IF A follower deviates from the leader's prescribed path, he is guilty of deviating from Jesus. This isn't the same as biblical confrontation, when someone first examines his heart, then prayerfully and kindly brings up another's sin. The intent of an abusive leader is to shame and ridicule followers into her prescribed program of holiness.

3. They Use Exclusive Language

THEY SAY, "WE'RE THE ONLY MINISTRY REALLY FOLLOWING JESUS," or "We have all the right theology." They truly believe that their way of doing things, thinking theologically, or handling ministry and church is the only correct way. Everyone else is wrong, misguided, or stupidly naive.

4. They Create a Culture of Fear and Shame

OFTEN THERE IS NO GRACE FOR SOMEONE WHO FAILS TO LIVE UP TO the church's or ministry's expectations. And if someone steps outside the often-unspoken rules, leaders shame him or her into compliance. Abusive leaders can't admit failure but often search out failure in others and use that knowledge to hold them in fear and captivity. They often quote scriptures about not touching God's anointed or bringing accusations against an elder. Yet they often confront sin in others, particularly ones who bring up legitimate biblical issues. Or they have their circle of influence take on this task, silencing critics.

5. They Often Have a Charismatic Leader at the Helm Who Starts Off Well but Slips into Arrogance, Protectionism, and Pride

A LEADER MAY START OFF BEING PERSONABLE AND INTERESTED IN others' issues, but he or she eventually withdraws to a small group of yes-people and isolates from the needs of others. The leader harbors a cult of personality. If the central figure of the ministry or church left, the entity would collapse because it depended entirely on one person to hold the place together. The ministry is geared toward this central figure in perpetrating the "machine" of ministry.

6. They Cultivate Dependence on One Leader for Spiritual Information

IN THESE SITUATIONS, PERSONAL DISCIPLESHIP ISN'T ENCOURaged. Often the Bible is pushed away to the fringes unless the main leader is teaching it, and only his or her perspective is honored as true. Questioning the leader is equated with questioning God.

7. They Demand Servanthood of Their Followers but Live Prestigious, Privileged Lives

THEY LIVE ALOOF FROM THEIR FOLLOWERS AND JUSTIFY THEIR extravagance as God's favor and approval on their ministry. Instead of obeying Jesus' instructions to take the last seat, they often take the first seat at events and court others to grant them privileges. They demand the best parking place, the prominent seat, a life of ease. After all, they've paid their dues and are now due honor.

8. They Buffer from Criticism by Placing People Around Themselves Whose Only Allegiance Is to the Leader

ABUSIVE LEADERS VIEW PEOPLE WHO BRING UP ISSUES AS ENEMIES. Those who were once friends or allies swiftly become combatants when a concern is raised. Sometimes these people who bring up honest issues are banished, told to be silent, or shamed into submission.

9. They Hold to Outward Performance but Reject Authentic Spirituality

ABUSIVE LEADERS ARE LIKE PHARISEES. THEY PLACE BURDENS ON followers to act a certain way, dress an acceptable way, and have an acceptable lifestyle. But they cannot live up to those expectations. They may preach about a harmonious family life, but behind the closed doors of their homes, they yell at their kids and intimidate their families with fear.

10. They Use Exclusivity for Allegiance

FOLLOWERS CLOSE TO THE LEADER FEEL LIKE INSIDERS—LIKE THEY have a special place in the leader's kingdom. This feeling empowers them to protect the leader because in protecting the leader, they're protecting their favored privileges. Everyone else is on the fringes, though longing to be in that inner circle. The inner circle's barrier tends to be impenetrable.

Ways to Cope

WHAT IF YOU'VE READ THIS LIST, NODDING YOUR HEAD AND FEELING duped? Recognizing where you are or where you've been is the first step toward healing and health. The enemy of your soul need not win this battle. You can be delivered from the evil one and the people he influences.

As someone who wants to live and emulate an uncaged life, I have thought a lot about what might be helpful for those of you walking through a difficult church or ministry situation. These ways of coping aren't exhaustive, but they're biblical.

Take Your Commitment Seriously

Too many times we take the convenient way out. If someone hurts us, we don't want to take the time to work through the issues in a healthy manner. God calls all of us to our local body of believers, and our covenant with those people (who are sinful just like us) is a serious, important one. We should not take lightly a desire to abandon the fellowship God has brought us to.

Ask God If It's Time to Confront

Matthew 18 delineates when we should confront and the manner in which we should. If we've been hurt by someone, we are to go to that person in private and share our perspective. If the person refuses to listen, we bring witnesses. And after that, the leaders of the church. Confronting in love is one of the hardest disciplines in the Christian life because it requires deep humility on our part (to take the log out of our own eyes first), and it is risky. When we dare to bring another's sin to light, we risk misunderstanding, slander, and all sorts of painful things. But if God calls you to bring up an abusive situation, you must obey. Not merely to maintain your peace of mind but to prevent other people from becoming victims of the perpetrator's behavior.

Refrain from Chatter

Gossip and hearsay destroy ministries and churches. Rise above both of them. Keep your circle small. While it's okay to discreetly search out a discerning friend to see whether you're crazy in the midst of an abusive situation, it's not okay to alert everyone. Keep things under wraps before, during, and after a confrontation. God's beautiful body is the church. We don't want to do anything that makes for disunity. (That is not to say we should avoid confrontation, but in doing so, we need to listen more than speak.)

Consider Stepping Away for a Time to Gain Perspective

Take time away to renew, refresh, and seek God to see what He has for you. Sometimes when you're in the midst of an abusive situation, you can't think clearly about it. Removing yourself from it for a period will help you clarify your position and give you time to heal.

Hold the Body of Christ in High Regard

As I mentioned earlier, God is zealous for His bride. Others will know we're Christians by our united love for each other. Satan's schemes are always to divide and bring disunity. Do not be privy to or a part of his ways. If you're deeply hurt, find a way for Jesus to shoulder that hurt. Seek counsel outside the church that's harmed you. And pray for the protection of that body. Don't contribute to its malaise.

Recognize That Sometimes You Have to Break Ties Permanently

If you've walked through most of these steps and still you sense God saying to move on, then do. Not with fanfare or ire or angry words. Once you've said what needs to be said to the right people, leave. Spend time working through your pain. Seek counseling. Ask God for discernment for the next ministry opportunity He places before you. And also be willing to be an agent of healing for others who may leave the abusive situation.

Notes

Chapter 1: "Pray Like This": Pray First

1. http://www.preceptaustin.org/matthew_67-8.htm.
2. W. E. Vine, *Vine's Complete Expository Dictionary* (Nashville: Thomas Nelson, 1996), s.v., "proskuneo," 745.
3. Shane Claiborne and Tony Campolo, *Red Letter Revolution* (Nashville: Thomas Nelson, 2012), 32.
4. "What to Fill Your Heart With," *Take on Torah*, September 22, 2011, http://takeontorah.blogspot.com/2011_09_01_archive.html.

Chapter 2: "Our Father in Heaven": Live in Your Father's Affection

1. W. E. Vine, *Vine's Complete Expository Dictionary* (Nashville: Thomas Nelson, 1996), s.v. "father," 228.
2. Sandra Glahn, *Mocha on the Mount* (Nashville: AMG Publishers, 2006), 57.
3. Commentary on Matthew 6:9–10, http://www.preceptaustin

.org/matthew_69-10.htm.
4. Vine, *Vine's Complete Expository Dictionary*, s.v. "abba," 1.
5. C. H. Spurgeon, "The Fatherhood of God," Spurgeon Archive, September 12, 1858, http://www.spurgeon.org/sermons/0213.htm.

Chapter 3: "May Your Name Be Kept Holy": Allow God to Be God

1. *Hagiastheto*, meaning "to see as holy or set apart." *Matthew 6:9–10 Commentary*, http://www.preceptaustin.org/matthew_69-10.htm.
2. Vine, *Vine's Complete Expository Dictionary*, s.v. "onoma," 425.
3. Nicholas Ayo, *The Lord's Prayer: A Survey Theological and Literary* (New York: Rowman & Littlefield, 2003), 37.
4. Stephen Mansfield, *ReChurch: Healing Your Way Back to the People of God* (Carol Stream, IL: Tyndale House, 2010), 15.
5. Ibid., 62.
6. "He'll Take Care of the Rest," http://www.youtube.com/watch?v=gAe0q21YgTQ.

Chapter 4: "May Your Kingdom Come Soon": Walk in the Great Right Now

1. Michael Card, "Things We Leave Behind."
2. For a more extensive understanding of the extremes of narcissism, read this article about the traits of narcissistic personality disorder, http://www.halcyon.com/jmashmun/npd/traits.html.

Chapter 6: "As It Is in Heaven": Let Heaven Frame Your Relationships

1. Michele Perry, *An Invitation to the Supernatural Life* (Minneapolis: Chosen Books, 2012), 125.

Chapter 7: "Give Us Today the Food We Need": Ask Jesus for Help

1. Shane Claiborne and Tony Campolo, *Red Letter Revolution* (Nashville: Thomas Nelson, 2012), 70, emphasis in original.

Chapter 8: "And Forgive Us Our Sins": Be Repentant

1. Oswald Chambers, "Christian Perfection," My Utmost for His Highest, http://www.oswaldchambers.co.uk/Readings.php?day=2&month=12&year=&language=English.
2. Michael Card, *Scribbling in the Sand: Christ and Creativity* (Downers Grove, IL: InterVarsity Press, 2002), 163.
3. H. R. Rookmaaker cited in *Scribbling in the Sand: Christ and Creativity* by Michael Card, 136–37.
4. Tim Challies, "In Which I Ask Ann Voskamp's Forgiveness," challies.com, May 28, 2012, http://www.challies.com/articles/in-which-i-ask-ann-voskamps-forgiveness.

Chapter 9: "As We Have Forgiven Those Who Sin Against Us": Defy Bitterness

1. Stephen Mansfield, *ReChurch: Healing Your Way Back to the People of God* (Carol Stream, IL: Tyndale House, 2010), 10.
2. Shane Claiborne and Tony Campolo, *Red Letter Revolution* (Nashville: Thomas Nelson, 2012), 62.
3. This story is fully recounted in my book *Thin Places: A Memoir* (Grand Rapids: Zondervan, 2010), 43–49.
4. Dietrich Bonhoeffer, *A Testament to Freedom: The Essential Writings of Dietrich Bonhoeffer*, ed. Geffrey B. Kelly and F. Burton Nelson (New York: HarperCollins, 1995), 308.
5. Catherine Claire Larson, *As We Forgive* (Grand Rapids: Zondervan, 2009),13.

Chapter 10: "And Don't Let Us Yield to Temptation": Dare to Engage Anyway

1. A. B. Simpson cited in *Streams in the Desert* by L. B. Cowman, ed. James Reimann (Grand Rapids: Zondervan, 1997), 119, March 18.

Chapter 11: "But Rescue Us from the Evil One": Be Fully Alive

1. Three excellent books on the subject include *The Power of Full Engagement* by Jim Loehr and Tony Schwartz (New York: Free Press, 2003); *The Rest of God* by Mark Buchanan (Nashville: W. Publishing Group, 2006); and *Margin* by Richard Swenson (Colorado Springs: NavPress, 2004).

About the Author

MARY DEMUTH IS AN AUTHOR AND SPEAKER WHO LOVES TO HELP people live uncaged, freedom-infused lives. She's the author of fifteen books, including six novels and her critically acclaimed memoir, *Thin Places*. After church planting in Southern France, Mary, her husband, and their three teenagers now live in a suburb of Dallas. Find out more at:

MARYDEMUTH.COM

WALLAROUNDYOURHEART.COM

#OPENHEART